POSITIVE PARENT CONFIDENT CHILD

Parenting Tips to Raise Happy, Confident and Successful Child

AMRITA NEOGI KUNDU

*For Reyansh
Gratitude, my dear son,
for converting me from a depressed to
a positive person and giving me the
strength to help other parents.*

For my husband, Sayan

*Thanks for your unconditional
love and support.*

Contents

About the Author

Amrita Neogi Kundu is an Indian writer and philanthropist. She served as an Assistant Professor in Electrical Engineering and guided many students over several years. She wrote an educational book for students. For her son, she soon developed a keen interest in self-development, behavioral science and psychology and started to research it. This book is a reflection of her experience and knowledge.

Introduction

In this competitive world, we, the parents, are very much concerned about our children. We worry a lot about 'what will happen next' to our children. Being worried, we decide to take actions that are good for our children. Sometimes we overburden our children, or sometimes we do not pay any attention to them, and then we expect them to give their utmost performance in study, dance, singing, drawing, and so on. Most of us pay little attention to our little ones' mind, and end up with lots of frustrations, assassinating our children's confidence and leaving them alone in the world as cowards, distrustful, lacking confidence.

So, getting good marks or winning lots of prizes in any event is not the aim of this book. This book will provide a guideline to build a confident, resilient, and happy child, so they can achieve success in their later life, possess good health, and enjoy their financial freedom.

Let's start…

Chapter 1

Understand the Child's Personality

We see some children are noisy and some are quiet. When one child cries loudly and blames others for the hurt he received, another child remains silent and refuses to talk. So, it is time to understand your child's personality and why he behaves the way he does. This helps parents to connect with their children. When the expectations placed upon a child are synchronised with his particular personality, the child experiences self-confidence and achieves greater happiness. According to German psychiatrist Carl Gustav Jung, there are 2 types of personalities: one is Introvert (introversion), and the other is Extrovert (extroversion). Let's have a look at which type your little one is –

Introvert

A child who possesses introvert characteristics is not always quiet; sometimes they become communicative and lively depending upon the situation. Here are some clues to help you to understand the characteristics of an introverted personality:

- Takes a wait-and-watch approach. Before entering a new situation, he observes well, thinks about it, and then slowly participates

- Enjoys being alone

- Enjoys one-on-one communication more than group talk

- Before joining the stage, first observes, talks, decides, and joins last

- Listens more, speaks less

- More reserved
- Shares ideas only when requested again and again
- Can appear anxious in new situations
- Needs time to recover from loud or overwhelming event
- Unable to express feelings properly
- Thinks before speaking
- Struggles with transitions
- Recharges when alone and enjoys solo tasks like drawing, playing with Legos, or playing music

How to Raise an Introverted Child

- **Respect their privacy:** Introverted children tend to have a very rich internal world. They love to spend time with their thoughts. Sometimes they do not want to include you in their inner world of thought. This does not indicate that they don't need you or that they disrespect you; it is just that they want to be alone. By letting them be as they are, you are sending a signal to them that you support their privacy and understand them well. Don't push your uncomfortable little one to join a large party. Be polite with them when there is a big, crowded event and talk about the event again and again, so they come to know what will happen there there and become comfortable. As an unknown situation may create anxiety for an introverted child.

- **Understand their feelings:** When your child is quiet and refuses to talk to you, just leave him alone at that moment. Introverted children need time and space to process their own emotions. You may notice this, for example, when your child comes back home from school upsets and refuses to talk. It is better to leave him be and talk later. You can give him a bunch of paper to write down or draw his thoughts. Tell him to make or draw an emoji that shows how he feels right now. Then, talk politely about his thoughts and discuss the problems. Tell him his feelings are natural, and there's no need to feel guilty. Assure him it's okay—it's a part of life. Just encourage introverted children to write about their feelings, as they are less expressive, tend to hide their true feelings, and think about others. The good news is that introverts enjoy writing more than discussion. Lots of talking drains their energy.

- **Allot solo play time:** Refusing playdates or avoiding joining a large group does not indicate that your little one is unsocialised. An introvert thrives when he is alone and playing with his favourite, cars, and Legos. This is not abnormal. For an introvert, a day at school is exhausting. So, when he returns home, he needs solo time to play by himself. That's why, before engaging your introverted child in different activities like dancing, playing cricket, learning music, swimming, etc., you should allot time for his solo play.

- **Value the decisions they make:** Introverted children often think and feel deeply. So, depending on their own values and thoughts, they make decisions about picking up their hobbies, music, and so on. These children have less tendency to follow others, and their decisions are unique. So, value their choices and support them instead of pushing them to do what others do.

- **Encourage them to socialise:** Don't push your introverted child to "go out and talk to people." Such children have difficulty in making new friends. In this case, role play is a good idea. Act as if you, teddy bears, dolls, and the toy tiger are all strangers, and tell him to talk with and introduce himself to the strangers. This encourages them to make new friends and helps to improve his speaking ability. If anything goes wrong in the play zone while your child is playing with others, don't scold him in front of everyone. Never embarrass him in public. This may lead your child to refuse further play and damage his self-confidence.

Extrovert

When you see your child talking a lot at home and outside, enjoying big parties, and feeling at ease communicating with strangers, congrats! You are raising an extroverted child.

Some qualities of extroverted children are:

- Enjoy big parties and gatherings
- Communicative
- Make friends easily
- Show ease in communicating with strangers
- Energised when they are surrounded by people
- Easily bored when alone
- Enjoy group tasks and group games like cricket, football, etc.
- Talk without thinking
- More likely to talk than listen
- Making decisions depending on others' opinions and considering external situations
- Give quick reactions without much thought
- Expressive and enthusiastic
- Process thoughts and emotions after they have done something

How to Raise an Extroverted Child

Raising extroverted children requires lots of care and patience so that children can thrive. Provide them with an environment that matches their personality, and watch how children become happy and confident.

- **Accept them as they are:** Yes, I know, extroverted children are talkative and very energetic. Please don't try to control it. Let them talk. Let them discuss their problems. Let them ask lots of questions. As they are often expressive, they can be overwhelmed by their emotions. So, handle it calmly. I know remaining calm when there are shouting children is a very difficult job. But you have to be. You have to accept that your child is an extrovert, and it is in his nature. Give your child some time to calm down, then discuss. Don't try to say anything when he is at the peak of his emotions. Assure him that you are always with him. Once your child reaches a calm state, then tell him what is right and what is wrong.

- **Help to channel their energy:** Energetic extroverts are outgoing by nature, so involve them in outdoor activities. As they are very good at teamwork, try to involve them in cricket, football, hockey, or other team sports. Before engaging your children, always ask if they are okay with sports that are restricted by rules and regulations because some extroverts are okay with regulations, and some are not. Involve extroverted children in crafting and building projects and talk during the process. Encourage them to complete the task they have started. Sometimes, they arrange small get-togethers with their friends to channel their energy.

- **Restrict distractions:** Sometimes, it is necessary to restrict distractions for extroverts. Unlimited distractions cause them to lose concentration. At such times, they don't understand how to channel their energy and may become aggressive. So, exposure to digital screens, "go and enjoy parties," and some outdoor activities should be restricted. Try to follow routines and set boundaries to keep them on the proper track.

- **Pay attention to active listening skills:** Children are talkative, so they listen less. To improve this skill, play active listening games with them. Tell them a story, ask questions about it, and give them points to show how good they are at listening. This way, we can instil listening ability in children. To improve concentration in study, practise mindfulness. Due to their "go-go" nature, children often suffer from a lack of concentration.

- **Teach them to cope with their emotions:** Extroverts always seek attention. If they don't get it, they may become anxious, depressed, or feel unwanted. Teach them that it is normal when someone refuses to talk or play. Teach them they cannot control others. Show them this to a reasonable point and then redirect their energy into useful work.

- **Introduce other sources for personal growth:** Extroverts gather knowledge from their constant social interactions. So, it is the parent's responsibility to introduce them to the value of learning from non-interactive sources at an early age. Encourage them to read books. Initially, introduce books with more pictures and fewer words.

Ambivert

An ambivert child is one who shows a combination of extroverted and introverted traits. When a child gets energy from being alone as well as from being with friends, then there is no doubt that the child lies in between extroverted and introverted personalities.

Here are some traits of an ambivert:

- Good listener and a good communicator
- Enjoys being alone as well as being surrounded by people
- Can be a good leader and a good follower
- Stable, consistent, and dependable
- Likes both structured and unstructured games
- Doesn't always understand what they want in alone time or with friends
- Likes to meet new people but not always
- Enjoys short conversations
- Comfortable in many different friend groups
- Empathetic
- Socialises a lot but values his own time

How to Raise an Ambivert Child

It may seem that raising an ambivert child is easy, but in reality, it is not. Like other personality traits, an ambivert has its own difficulties. An ambivert sometimes does not understand what he wants at a particular moment and becomes restless.

- **Rethink your child's misbehaviour:** With an ambivert child, it is seen that sometimes he behaves properly with his uncle, and sometimes he simply refuses to talk. This creates an embarrassing situation. Parents become frustrated and angry and start to scold. Instead of scolding, try to understand that your child is an ambivert. An ambivert child behaves according to his mood. Sometimes an ambivert will talk to a stranger with ease, and sometimes he is reserved. It is not abnormal. This indicates that your ambivert child needs downtime and wants to spend time alone. So, your support is necessary. Always remember your support is the strength of your child.

You can also observe that when there is a party, your little one enjoys a lot with his friends but not until the end. In the middle of the party, he becomes upset or restless and wants to go back home. Don't scold him. It happens because he belongs to the ambivert category. So, it is better to allow him "me-time" to feel re-energised.

- **How ambiverts feel and what they want to do:** Help your ambivert understand their feelings. It is better to give them a journal and tell them to write down their feelings at that moment and to think about what they want to do. This process helps them to understand their feelings and provides an opportunity to decide whether they want to play with friends or need some time alone. I faced such problems very often when I went to parties with my son, and every time, the party ended with chaos created by him. But when I understood my son's nature, I always tried to leave the party early. Being unaware of ambivert's feelings, an ambivert becomes either restless and loud or ambiverts become worried. Being balanced by nature and finding peace can be exhausting for an ambivert. They should learn to focus on their own needs, not others.

- **Make them independent:** As ambiverts are dependable, to make them independent, give some authority so they can make their own decisions. Too much independence can cause stress and pressure for your little one, so intervention is needed in some cases.

Time to act

So, extroversion, introversion, and ambiversion are the initial tiny steps to understand our child well. This will help us to reduce our expectations from our child and also provide a concept of how to handle our little one without damaging his self-confidence. The ultimate aim is to raise a confident and happy child who can handle the harsh world smoothly. Always remember, no one remains 100% introverted or 100% extroverted throughout their life. Environment, social influence, and friend circles are the main causes of changes in one's personality. Your little one, who is now an introvert, may show extroverted personality traits later in life.

Hope this chapter will help you to know your child well and to stop immediately comparing your child with others, as each belongs to different personality traits.

Now it is time to act according to.............................

Chapter 2

Establish Strong Bonding and Enhancing Different Skills

Chini, a six-year-old girl, often shouted and complained about her food. One day she simply refused to eat breakfast as it was *upma*, which she did not like. She cried, shouted, and demanded noodles, her favourite dish. Her mother said she would make it another day, but there were no changes in Chini's attitude. At last, her mother became furious and scolded her badly, and things ended up in a mess.

This situation often creates frustration among parents. They don't understand how to control the whole situation peacefully, and it ends in trauma.

Parents are very good about their children's health. They know when to give healthy food, give medicine if their children are sick, help children to maintain good sleep, and so on. But they often ignore the mental health of their children. If they pay keen attention to the inside of their children's minds, they can explore a lot about their children.

Paying attention to the mental health of a child does not reduce the stress of parenting, but it definitely helps to set up a strong connection between you and your little one and boosts their confidence level.

Now, one should understand how a child's brain reacts to stimulations and how to tame it. Let's start by looking at how the brain functions.

Brain Rules on Emotions and Behaviours

The brain is the most important and complex part of our bodies. If we know how the brain functions in relation to our emotions and behaviours, it will be easier to handle any situation we face. The largest part of the brain is the cerebral cortex. It is the outer portion of the brain and can be broken into 4 parts: the frontal lobe, parietal lobe, temporal lobe, and occipital lobe. The frontal lobe is at the front of the head and is responsible for logical thinking, speech, reasoning, and managing emotions. It is also known as the 'higher brain' or 'rational brain'.

On the other hand, the part of the brain that controls and processes emotions and memories is known as the limbic system. It is directly underneath the temporal lobe. The significant parts of this system are the amygdala, hypothalamus, and hippocampus. The amygdala is responsible for controlling and regulating emotions such as rage, anger, fear, and pleasure. It also plays a significant role in forming strong memories. If the amygdala finds anything threatening, it sends a signal to the hypothalamus. The hypothalamus is the most active and well-connected part. It processes signals coming from the amygdala or from every sensory part and reroutes them to specific areas throughout the brain. It is mainly responsible for making our body's 'fight-or-flight' response. The 'fight-or-flight' response is when our body decides to escape (flight) from a situation or to defend (fight) ourselves. Lastly, the hippocampus is the part responsible for converting our short-term memory to long-term memory. Together, these 3 parts of the limbic system form the 'emotional brain'.

When a child is born, his brain size is only 25% of an adult's brain. The main structures of the brain are there, but the connections between the 'logical brain' and 'emotional brain' are not well-formed. In the first 5 years of life, connections are formed through experiences and emotional interactions with others. Every new experience creates new neural connections, and when the experience is repeated again and again, those connections become stronger.

At the time of birth, a child has a strongly developed 'emotional brain' because it provides survival thinking. It prompts actions without thought, either to 'escape' or 'fight', to keep us safe and secure.

But the 'rational brain' develops slowly, forming connections gradually. It is the most sophisticated part for solving problems, rational thinking, logic, planning, decision-making, and self-control. It makes new connections through experiences gained during childhood and adolescence. It is considered mature when we reach our mid-twenties.

So, when children throw tantrums because they are not given what they want, the wrong food, or someone has broken their favourite toys, this indicates that only the 'emotional brain' is active. They do not know how to operate the 'rational brain' as it is still learning how to manage these situations. Children's overwhelming emotions only trigger the 'emotional brain' to respond with the 'fight-or-flight' reaction. In this situation, by providing positive experiences, new neural connections are made between the 'emotional brain' and the 'rational brain', and the child learns how to control these situations. Gradually, children learn to control themselves. So, during a tantrum, parents or other caregivers must provide positive experiences rather than negative reactions, detachment, or overreaction.

I hope the above discussion provides an idea of how a little one's brain functions.

Now it is time to consider situations that we want to control positively to bring up our offspring confidently.

LIMBIC SYSTEM

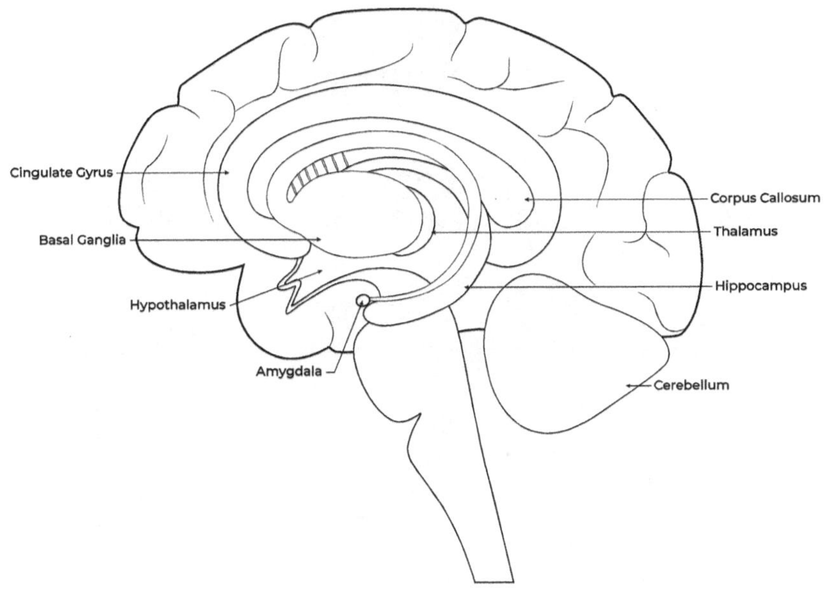

HUMAN BRAIN

Frontal lobe
Parietal lobe
Occipital lobe
Temporal lobe
Cerebellum
Spinal Cord

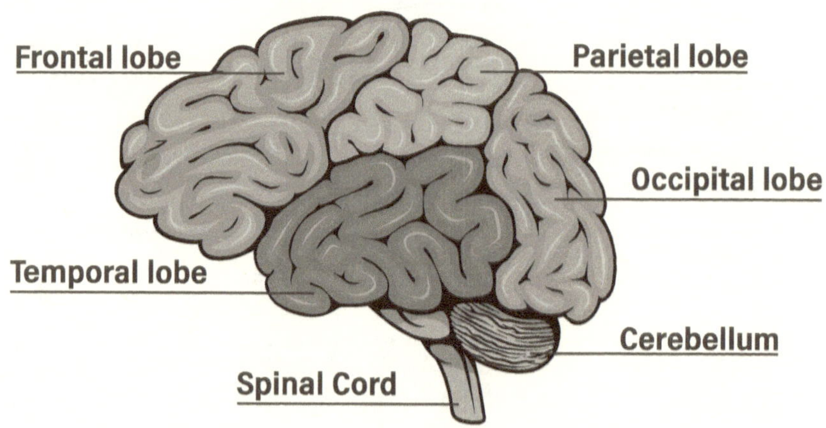

A. First Connect With Emotion, Then Discuss

To control someone, they must first be convinced, much like what happens in the process of hypnotising. The same applies if you want to teach your child. When Chini was crying for noodles, her mother should have connected emotionally first, then discussed the problem. Her mother should hug her and support her emotions, as her feelings, being too strong, simply deny all logical thinking. Soothe her by saying, 'Yes, you are right. Noodles are tasty. If we eat noodles, it will be fun for both of us.' This helps Chini's brain to understand that her mother recognises her feelings. Once she calms down, her mother can then convince her to have upma and ask if there is something more she would like to enjoy with noodles tomorrow. Giving her some positive experiences rather than negative emotions (such as scolding or punishing) helps her understand the situation, and she will learn to control her emotions.

B. The Power of Storytelling

The impact of 'storytelling' is so strong that we can still remember the childhood stories told by our parents or grandparents. Some moral stories with life lessons have a great impact on forming our character. Listening to autobiographies helps us cope with different situations. So, the power of storytelling, whether by oneself or by others, has a great effect on shaping a child's mental health (psychological) and behaviour. Let's find out what the hidden powers (skills) can be developed through storytelling.

- **Cognitive Development**

As human minds love to listen to or share stories, there is no exception with a child. A child also loves to listen to stories. When a child converts the language of a story into a fantastic image in his mind, his imagination power is developed. Thus, storytelling helps children to improve their imagination, creativity, visual cognition, language, and problem-solving skills.

'Neural Coupling' occurs between a listener and a storyteller as similar parts of their brains are engaged during this process. So, if the storyteller is the mother and the listener is her little one, naturally a 'neural coupling' is formed between them. It creates a strong bond between the mother and her child. When the brain sees or hears a story, its neurons fire in the same patterns as the speaker's brain, and as a consequence, neural coupling is formed.

When a child asks questions about the story, it indicates that the child's logical brain is in action. This helps a child to think independently, increases curiosity, and above all, allows him to express his own opinions.

- **Increase in listening and comprehension capability**

Children are often restless and unable to pay attention to a single thing for a long time. Listening to stories helps them to focus. When they pay attention to a story, they develop the ability to comprehend and concentrate on a crucial subject.

- **Development of speaking capability**

Telling stories improves one's speaking capability and also helps in acquiring knowledge on language. When a child tells a story about what happened at school, on the playground, and so on, he becomes more confident in expressing his feelings in language. Thus, gradually, a child can easily express his feelings and develops knowledge on language.

- **Emotional development**

Stories teach children to identify different emotions like happiness, excitement, anger, sadness, disgust, surprise, irritation, love, and fear. Stories build a strong emotional library for a child. When a child feels sympathy for the hero or shows anger toward the villain of a story, it indicates that he is learning about different emotions and is able to express them.

- **Development of social skills**

When children listen to stories, they not only enrich their emotions, language, and vocabulary, but also gain non-verbal communication and other social skills. Children understand different types of body language, which helps them to become good communicators. Thus, children gradually develop various social skills, such as communicating clearly, understanding others' emotions and body language, listening carefully, cooperating with others, giving constructive feedback, helping others like their favourite story heroes, sharing things, making eye contact while communicating, following directions, and so on.

For those who struggle with making friends, 'storytelling' by a parent helps them deal with negative social situations and build meaningful relationships with others.

- **Development of Intelligence**

According to psychology, intelligence is the ability to acquire knowledge from experience, adapt to new situations, and use knowledge to manipulate desired outcomes in one's environment.

Yes, it is true that by listening to different stories, a child (kid) develops his intelligence. He can handle new situations with ease. Stories have an impact on our emotions, and most decisions are made by our emotional mind rather than the logical mind, often without us being aware of it. When a speaker tells a story, the child easily connects his brain to the speaker's brain, envisions the story rather than focusing on dates, acquires knowledge from the story, and ultimately applies this knowledge to manipulate his adverse environment to achieve positive outcomes.

- **Widening the Worldview**

There are different types of stories available in the market. Some stories provide concepts outside of our society, teaching the child to respect others who do not belong to our society.

The child learns to understand and respect other cultures, which is necessary to become a happy and successful human being.

- **Increase Memory**

When the speaker asks the little listener questions about the story, and the listener answers with curiosity and explains more, this simply indicates that memory is boosting. Recalling something from the storage of our brain (i.e. 'short-term memory') is in progress. After 2 or more months, when the little one can still remember those things that seemed interesting to him (emotionally impactful), it indicates that his 'long-term memory' is sharpening. So, in one sentence, stories create emotions. Researchers have found that stories are sources of emotions and memories.

- **Improving Bonding**

It is often seen that when great speakers give their speeches, they use stories to connect with their audience. They also provide more stories than data to make their speeches more interesting, and they successfully hold the attention of the audience. This is also true for our little listeners.

So, storytelling helps parents to grab the attention of children, allowing both to spend quality time together. Spending quality time undoubtedly strengthens the bond between parent and child. It also fosters emotional connections and attachment.

- **Changing Life**

Some stories have such a great impact on the mind that they can change a person completely. For example, when a boy listens to a story about wildlife and it touches his emotions, it may change his life. Later in life, he might become a national wildlife photographer, an animal rescuer, or a veterinary surgeon.

Thus, stories can change our lifestyle and help us to find out the right career path according to our interests. Different types of stories also help individuals discover their true intentions and motivate them to change their lives for the betterment of themselves and others.

C. Teaching Empathy

When my son was in pre-school, he used to cry daily. To calm him, my husband told him, 'I am just downstairs from your school, looking after our car so that no one can steal it. You'll see my face first when the school door opens.' After one day, my little one somehow managed to stop crying. The following week, a little boy, new to the school, cried when his parent left. At that time, my son went to him and soothed him by saying, 'Don't worry, your mum is just downstairs and waiting for you. She will pick you up when school is over.' (As described by his teacher). This incident shows empathy.

Empathy is necessary to maintain good interpersonal relationships. It helps us to form strong bonds with parents, siblings, peers, and spouses. Therefore, an empathetic child becomes socially successful as he grows into adulthood. Empathy also aids in the learning process and helps a child to achieve good marks in the field of education. It teaches a child to act according to situations and helps him to overcome negative situations such as teasing and bullying at school.

Sometimes you can see some children uprooting small plants, and have on feelings on the other hand, some children feel sorrow for the uprooted plants, why does this happen? The children who are taught about empathy feel sorrow. Every child comes into this world with some level of empathy, and with proper guidance, a child becomes an empathetic adult in the future. Children take cues from us and learn to show empathy. When our child cries, we soothe him; when our little one gets hurt, we take care of him; when a family member is upset, we also try to help her etc. These are examples of the first steps in teaching empathy to children. If a child is taught that plants have life and that if you uproot or tear any leaf from a plant, it gets hurt and feels the same as you would if someone hurts you, he begins to understand empathy. I am often surprised to watch some parents allow their children to uproot plants and tear flowers and leaves.

In such cases, parents remain silent. However, when children's empathy is needed in certain situations, and they do not show it, parents become frustrated and rebuke their children for not showing empathy. This is a bad idea. A lack of empathy in any child is not his fault; it is simply a lack of proper nurturing by his caregivers (teachers, parents, grandparents).

D. Teach Self-dependence

Self-dependent people are those who are emotionally stable and confront life's hurdles on their own. They think and make decisions independently. 'Self-reliance' or 'self-dependence' means not worrying about 'what others say,' and this approach to life leads to happiness. Thus, a self-dependent child grows into a happy adult who can easily handle life's challenges. As the saying goes, 'Rome wasn't built in a day,' similarly, the quality of 'self-reliance' or 'self-dependence' will not develop overnight. It requires patience, empathy, and time.

Here are some simple steps for developing the quality of 'self-reliance':

- **Assign Responsibility**

Parents can assign simple tasks to their children, such as arranging toys in the proper place, making their beds, bringing their books and notebooks at study time, filling water bottles from water purifiers, and so on. A child becomes confident when he accomplishes such tasks and hear a 'thank you' from his parents.

Always remember that an excessive number of tasks (responsibilities) may burden on your child.

As the child grows, assign slightly more difficult tasks, such as asking him to help wash the car, to assist you in kitchen or laundry work, and so on.

Thus, a child can understand his capabilities and develops a sense of self-dependency.

- **Separation of Tasks**

According to Austrian psychiatrist Alfred Adler, the separation of tasks is necessary to reduce one's burden. Suppose cooking is the wife's responsibility; then the husband should not interfere in cooking but the only thing he can do just to assist his wife. 'Interference' and 'assistance' are not the same. When the husband tells the wife how to cook perfectly, where to keep food, where to throw vegetable peels, and monitors her every step, these are nothing but interference. In this case, she has no freedom in doing her task. On the other hand, when the husband helps the wife by cutting vegetables, boiling milk, or setting the table, these are examples of 'assistance' to make the whole kitchen work quicker and faster.

The same applies to our children's lives. 'Studying' is the task of the child. However, parents often intrude and make their child's life miserable. Yes, of course, parents must guide their children, as it is their responsibility, but creating pressure on the child's life is a bad thing, which is often done by parents. Parents may expect their child to get into a good university, a good school, or to win a prize by holding a top position in class. These are simple expectations from parents, but they often think about what others will say if their child doesn't get into a prestigious school, and so on. According to Adler's psychology, tasks should be divided simply. 'Studying' is the child's task, and he has to do it. The only thing parents can do is just assist him. Thus, scolding the child for not performing well in class is just interfering with his life. If the child performs poorly, he has to face the consequences. It is the parent's duty to tell the child that 'studying' is his task and he has to do it, or else he will suffer the consequences. Parents should explain the consequences elaborately so that the child can understand the impotence of his task.

Thus, children will be able to understand their responsibility.

• Be Patient and Don't Be a Perfectionist

It takes great patience to sit back and watch children perform their assigned tasks. When a child performs a task, he makes a lot of mess and takes a lot of time. 'Mess' and 'time' are both intolerable for parents. But if you control yourself, your child will have more opportunity to learn to be self-dependent. Suppose your child is filling a water bottle, and you see that he spills water here and there, forget where he has kept the lid after filling it, struggles to put the lid on the bottle, and flood the kitchen floor. At this moment, you should control your nerves, stay calm, and refrain from intervening. When the child comes to you with the bottle filled with water, you should say, patting him on the back, 'Thank you, you've done a great job.' No scolding, no rebuking. Stay calm and serene. This attitude of yours gives your child the strength to become more self-reliant.

No one is perfect, and neither are our tasks. Always remember that a task performed by an adult will be much more perfect than one performed by a toddler. Therefore, parents need not to be perfectionists when it comes to their children's tasks. Always remember that 'perfection' is limitless. There is always someone better at performing certain tasks than you. So, value the Japanese word *wabi-sabi*, which means an aesthetic that finds beauty in things imperfect, incomplete, and not permanent.

• Value Money

Financial independence is necessary for a self-sufficient person. From childhood, parents should teach about the value of money. Most parents avoid this lesson. Parents refuse to talk about money and do not allow children to handle it. If proper guidance is provided from childhood, handling money in adulthood will be easier. Even in school, financial knowledge is not provided, so it is the parents' responsibility to teach how to handle money efficiently. For example, parents should give pocket money to their children when they are about 10 years old, with the instruction to "spend only when you need to." Thus, unnecessary spending and borrowing will be reduced in adulthood, and the child will become more financially strong, which is necessary for independence.

So, if you become more patient, invest your valuable time, and let go of perfection, your child will become more confident, capable, responsible, and independent.

E. Help to Gather Knowledge Quickly

Some parents allow their children to watch videos (mainly on YouTube), and some do not. These parents believe watching YouTube or TV hampers the concentration level of the children. Sometimes, children start to act according to their favourite cartoon heroes, showing disapproval of studying or other tasks. Watching videos for too long may be harmful to the eyes and brain as well.

I believe that, to some extent, watching videos is not harmful at all, but the content of the videos must be positive and constructive.

It is seen that children can remember things more effectively when they are presented in video rather than in written form. Have you thought about why this happens?

Let's find the cause…

How the Brain Remembers

One most important thing is that our attention is also controlled by our brain. It decides what we pay attention to and what we do not. So, naturally, if something seems interesting to our brain, we pay attention to it and remember it with the help of our short-term memory. The brain cannot pay attention to boring things. When something becomes boring, it feels difficult to remember, and we yawn.

When we learn something new and complex, it always seems difficult because new neural connections are made inside our brain, and it takes some time. By doing one thing repeatedly—what we call practice—we solidify those new neural connections, and once these connections are strengthened, they are stored in our long-term memory. This is why we can remember the multiplication table of 2 instantly.

According to Ebbinghaus, a German psychologist, memory loss occurs within 1 or 2 hours after learning something, and it can be reduced by deliberate repetition.

For each letter or number, a neural connection is required, and that is why a page full of letters and numbers is hard to remember. Supposed to read the word "bat," the brain has to fetch the single letter "b" from its stored location, then "a," and then "t," and finally combine all 3 letters into an understandable form.

So, in our textbooks, having lots of information in written format makes it hard to learn and remember.

But in a picture or in a video, although there is a lot of information regarding colours, shapes, figures, movements, and so on, our brain sees it as a whole and, being interesting, pays full attention to it. Thus, pictures and videos are easier to remember as they are stored automatically in our brain, and our strong emotions help to form strong neural connections. As I have mentioned earlier, emotion creates memory.

So, if we try to teach our children through educational videos, their strong emotions capture their attention and help them to remember those information easily. Suppose you try to teach the solar system to your child; it is better to let him watch a video on it rather than giving a detailed theoretical explanation. Once the concept is clearly understood by your child, you may then go through the detailed theoretical explanation.

Allow Moderate Time to Watch Constructive Videos

I personally allow my son to watch "YouTube Kids" videos, and of course, those are positive, constructive, and educational. One day, my son came and asked me, 'Do you know how our modern latrine system works?' I replied, 'No,' and asked, 'Can you explain it?' He said confidently, 'Yes,' and immediately sat on the mat with his whiteboard and marker. Next, he gave a detailed explanation, which was correct. He said he learned it from 'The Fixies.' In this way, he learns a lot about different car constructions and their functions, making trucks with empty matchboxes, some paper crafts, and so on.

Watching positive YouTube videos for moderate amounts of time is not harmful. It also helps to identify children's interests.

However, allowing children to watch videos with adult content, violence, or destructive themes is harmful to their mental growth. They may become violent, feel a lot of mental pressure, misbehave with others, and so on. So, time limits and parental monitoring of videos are necessary. During the pandemic, I allowed my son to watch a TV show named *Chhota Bheem*. Soon I realised that my son thought of himself as *Bheem* and fought with his playmates like *Bheem* if anything went wrong with him. I immediately stopped him from watching that Chhota Bheem show and kept explaining, repeatedly, what was right and what was wrong about his activities with his friends. After some time, he gradually understood, and now he is a changed boy.

So, choosing proper video content is important as it has a strong impact on our mind.

There are some drawbacks to watching videos as well. Too much screen time creates lethargy towards studying, outdoor activities, and some crucial tasks, and it may cause some behavioural issues like talking rudely or crying. Excessive screen exposure may cause itchy and watery eyes.

Now it is your turn either to choose proper videos for your little one or to avoid watching videos.

Chapter 3

Find and Nurture Passion

Passion refers to a strong feeling of excitement either for something or about doing something. We often hear the word "passion" from popular actors, who say that acting is their passion; some cricketers have also mentioned that from childhood, cricket was their passion. They follow their passion, choose it as their career, and eventually succeed. As we are naturally influenced by popular figures, we parents become anxious to find our child's passion. If a child shows interest in soccer, then we, as parents, think it is his passion and force him to pursue soccer at any cost. But, in reality, "passion" may change year to year, month to month, week to week, or even day to day, like the weather.

My six-year-old son had a passion for playing cricket, so we soon enrolled him in a cricket academy. For the first few months, he enjoyed it a lot. At that time, he was a preschooler. Soon he started Grade I, and his school hours increased. He had to wake up early in the morning. He reached school at 7:30 a.m. and came back home around 1 p.m. After returning home, he had to finish his bath, play with his favourite cars, have his meal, and finally take some rest, i.e., a power nap. Then, when the clock struck 4 in the afternoon, he had to reach the playground for cricket. This was his regular routine. He returned home from the playground around 7 p.m., after which he had to finish his school homework. This hectic schedule exhausted my son. Soon, he felt the pressure and refused to go to the playground. Another reason for his loss of interest in cricket was a coach who often used offensive words and insulted children. Naturally, my little son stopped showing interest in cricket. Yes, we had spent money on the kit, but we had to support our son at any cost. We never pushed him to go to the field again. Thus, his first passion was buried under pressure.

Always remember, when our child takes admission in structured games, dance, and so on, it is not an easy task. There are lots of rules and regulations in any structured activity. Non-structured activities always provide free space to think, help them learn independently, and create opportunities. You often observe your child playing freely with peers, more happily than in any structured game.

Some parents worry if they do not find any particular interest in their children. They desperately try to discover a child's interest, and if they fail, they force their children to take admission as per their own interests. This attitude from parents creates stress and burden on the little one. Children may become rebellious by crying, showing anger, refusing to complete their homework, and so on. They begin to see their parents as oppressors.

Parents are the shelter of a child, but when they force him to do only what they want, the child becomes rebellious. This has an intense psychological impact on the child's mind, which can continue throughout life. So, it is "OK" if your child has no specific interest. As the child grows up, there is a probability to develop new interests, and he will definitely come to you to share them. So, don't be a tyrant; be a benefactor to your child.

Sometimes, a child shows interest in more than one field, like dancing, drawing, cooking, playing badminton, and so on. To excel in all fields, parents often decide to enrol the child in different professional courses. As a result, the child becomes exhausted and refuses to pursue any of them. I know a boy named Rahul who was interested in dancing and drawing. His mother decided to enrol him in a professional hip-hop dance academy and to an art class. She did so. Soon Rahul became exhausted but could not talk about it to his parents, as he saw them as oppressors. On weekends, he had to go to his dance academy to pursue his parents' dream. Once Katie Hurley, in her book *The Happy Kid Handbook,* mentions that "The best way to extinguish passion is to burn out your child."

A child needs free time to explore the world. Too much engagement creates too much pressure. Give them free space to grow; there is no need for professional and structured classes to pursue a passion. There is no need to be perfect. Simply being happy to do something, whether perfect or not, is the core of passion. If someone wants to convert his passion into a career, he will automatically take on the pressure. Parental intervention is not necessary.

My son loves to draw his dump trucks, excavators, bulldozers, trains, buses, cars, and other vehicles on a whiteboard with markers. I felt that he would excel with some proper guidance, so I enrolled him in an art class. However, his art teacher had a fondness for drawing human figures, which my son completely disliked. Art class also ended with a lot of frustration. Now, he is happy again with his whiteboard and colourful markers. Yes, I allowed him to leave the structured drawing class, and he still enjoys drawing at home, where he feels free.

Too many regulations take away children's freedom, and they naturally refuse to continue those activities.

I acknowledge that I am not perfect. I have learned a lot through my son and realised that childhood is a time for exploration and trying new things. It is full of fun and enjoyment.

Harsh words also drive attention away from one's passion. Scolding, rebuking, and beating are not helpful in continuing one's passion. These cause a lack of interest. Children try to excel in every field to fulfil their parents' desires, but when they see their parents criticising them, they feel a lot of pressure, and depression overshadows their mind. So, reprimanding is not a way to increase one's interest; rather, it causes withdrawal of interest.

Passion requires money, time, and patience. When my son refused to go to the cricket playground, my husband was offended as he had spent a lot of money on it. Of course, some passions are expensive and others are not. When your little one wants to play tennis, he needs a court, net, racket, and balls, which are expensive. But if your little one wants to join an art class for drawing, he only needs a sketchbook, pencil, eraser, and colours. So, tennis is more expensive than drawing. Once, my brother decided to learn guitar, but soon he lost interest and moved on. Now, his professional guitar is in the corner of the room.

As pursuing an interest requires time and patience, most children soon move on to their next interest. Children are lively and fickle. They easily lose interest in a particular activity. But as parents, we should stand by them, plan to save money for their passion, and definitely be "OK" if they move on.

Finding passion is like research in a scientific laboratory. If scientists succeed, they are rewarded; if not, there is nothing but a loss of money, time, and energy.

Sometimes parents forget that their passions are not the same as their children's passions. Just as all fingers are not the same, all children are different from each other. One child's interest is completely different from another child's interest. Parents often compare their children to others and set targets for them, which makes the children's life miserable. Provoked by society, parents decide to make decisions for their children and set targets for them. As a result, anxiety, stress, and illness are seen in children. A depressed child can't concentrate on anything once he was excellent at and starts to find negative aspects in everything. Perhaps your daughter is good at drawing, while her friend is good at dancing. That's OK. Allow her to draw. Help her to try new paintings. Praise her to give her the courage to continue her passion. Please don't enroll her in a dance class just because her friend is doing so.

Children are happier and more self-reliant when they are allowed to do what they love. This is the key to reducing stress hormones in our children's lives.

Steps for Finding and Nurturing Passion

- **Listen**

The first step to finding your little one's passion is to listen. Listen to what your child is saying about what he wants to do or what he hates to do. My son regularly said that he hated his drawing class, where he had to draw human figures, colour, and so on. But he loved to draw cars and trains on a whiteboard, as I discussed before. I misinterpreted this and enrolled him in an art class, which ended in a mess. So, listening to your child is an important part of discovering passion for your offspring. Sometimes, talking about children's dislike of certain tasks gives you a clue about what not to choose as their passion. So, it is a parent's duty to listen and interpret what children say and make the right decision for them.

- **Give Free Time**

Give sufficient free time to your children to discover their passion. If there is no such space, passion cannot develop.

Too much engagement leads to burnout of a child. The child becomes exhausted and seeks a break. It is better to engage in one activity per season. For example, swimming could be the activity for the summer season. So, involve your child in such seasonal activities and leave sufficient free time for him to explore his strengths and passions as well. If you keenly observe what a child does in his free time, you will easily find his interest.

- **Choose Words Carefully**

Parents should not use any harsh or negative words about their children's passion, as this damages their self-esteem. If a boy is interested in sewing, don't underestimate him. Who knows? One day, this little boy could become a popular fashion designer like Sabyasachi Mukherjee. According to outdated societal beliefs, don't tell him, 'Look, that's a girl's work.'

Your harsh or negative words may cripple him from showing interest, and our future fashion designer would be lost in this chaotic world.

Always encourage children to follow their interests. Always keep in mind that passion can change day by day, like the weather. Very few are lucky enough to pursue their passion with the support they receive from their parents. Be the parent of that lucky one.

- **Comparison is Not Allowed**

One day, I unconsciously praised a boy who is my son's friend. I mentioned that the boy was very good at doing planks and could hold the plank position for 3 minutes. Upon hearing this, my son suddenly started doing plank, and I was so surprised to see him doing it. Every child wants to occupy their parent's heart. If their parents show fondness for others, they may feel jealous. I know it is not a good feeling, but they are too young to understand this feeling of jealousy. So, try not to praise others' passions in front of your emotional child, especially when that child is your little one's friend. An emotional child quickly picks up on feelings of being unwanted and tries to pursue passions that are not his own. Thus, the true feeling of love remains untouched for these types of children.

On the other hand, some children thrive in competitive environments. They can find their true passion by chasing others' passions. But never encourage this competitive mindset, as it is a leading cause of depression in children. As soon as you recognise this, intervene quickly and try to boost your children's confidence. Comparison is harmful and stressful for children. Parents try to motivate them, but they can easily become victims of comparison. Just as every flower in the garden is different, so are the children. Be aware of this and don't bury children's passion under comparison.

My mother often compared me with my cousin. She used to say that she (my cousin) was better at studying, dancing, acting, and so on. At that time, I felt useless. I tried hard to please my mum, but, you know, chasing someone is a foolish task. You will never be happy. My mother never understood that each person has a unique quality that is definitely different from others. She never tried to find my strengths. From childhood until 2 years ago, I suffered from a lack of interest in doing anything, that we may call a passion. But now, I am happy to have found it, and it is writing. My happiness lies in sharing experiences and knowledge with others. Yes, now I can tell anyone that writing and reading are my passions. So, stop comparing and help your child to find his passion. If you are also suffering from a lack of interest in doing something, try following the next steps for both you and your child.

- **Ask Questions**

Some children talk a lot, while others remain quiet. These tips are mainly applicable to those who do not talk much. Talkative children often share what they love to do, what makes them sad, what they do not want to do, and so much more. But the quiet ones keep everything inside their minds.

So, it is better to ask questions to understand what they enjoy very much. Here are some questions that parents may ask to identify their child's 'passion.'

These questions include:

i. What makes you happy?

ii. What is your best moment?

iii. What is the thing that makes you sad?

iv. If you are allowed to play, what would you prefer to play?

v. What makes school fun for you?

vi. What do you hate most about school?

vii. Do you enjoy playing with your peers?

viii. Which do you enjoy most: drawing, dancing, cooking, or playing badminton?

ix. How do you want to spend your summer vacation?

x. What is your favourite book and why?

In addition to these questions, parents may ask him questions according to the situation, and if they are attentive, they can certainly find the areas of their children's interests.

Another positive aspect of asking questions is that it help to build a bond between you and your child. The child begins to believe that you care about him.

- **Show only the positive side**

When your child fails to win a prize in a dance competition and she is exceptionally good at dancing, don't criticise her. She dances because she loves it, so encourage her. Tell her it is a part of life. Failure doesn't mean giving up; it simply indicates there is room for improvement. If you are not concerned with winning, then your child will not worry about winning or losing the competition. Don't pass your tension onto your child. Let them enjoy what they love doing. One can flourish when one can see the positive, even in a bleak situation. If you have a positive mindset, then your child will emulate you, as children often follow their parents. Hopefully, he will continue his passion, even if he fails to succeed in it. Always remember to allow your little one to do what he loves. Do what makes both you and your child happy and refreshed. Life is not about winning or losing a competition; it is a journey with many good and bad memories.

- **Save money to spend**

In middle-class society, when a child is born, parents start saving money for higher education. No one thinks about passion. But passion is essential for mental development, and it is necessary to spend money to follow one's passion. Passions like knitting, cooking, drawing, and building structures with Lego require a small amount of money, but learning professional guitar, joining a professional hockey course, or learning computer programming can be more expensive. So, parents should set aside a portion of their savings to support their children's passions. It is true that when we achieve something, our focus often shifts toward something new. The same thing happens to our little ones. After gaining knowledge in a particular activity, a child may feel it's enough and want to try new things. They continue exploring until they find the perfect pursuit for their own soul. The same process applies to adults as well, as Robin Sharma describes in his book *The Monk Who Sold His Ferrari*. Searching for and trying new things is a natural part of life in the quest for happiness. Suppose a child loves to travel; then parents should save money to support this dream at least once a year. Perhaps one day, your little one will start a travel company that offers low-budget holiday plans for people.

- **Allow them to be bored**

As I mentioned earlier, my son had an interest in playing cricket and then drawing, but both ended up in a mess. So, my husband and I decided not to enrol him in any activities until he showed his own interest. We allow him to be bored and discover his strengths. My son is happy when he builds intricate Lego buildings, vehicles, robots, and bridges without any directions or help. He creates useful things from scraps. After making something new, he becomes so happy each time that he sings and dances around the room. Although he was able to make complex structures at the age of 3, somehow, overlooking this was a mistake on my part.

Boredom allows the invention of new activities. Some parents switch on the TV or hand over a mobile to let their children watch YouTube to get some free time for themselves. But it's healthier to allow our children to be bored so that their inner spark comes out.

- **Spend quality time**

Children are not objects. They expect you to spend time with them. They expect parents to play. So, try to find time to talk and play with your child. Yes, I know it's hard to find time while managing household and other chores. But for the sake of your child, and for his mental growth, you must try. When children enter their teenage years, they will never request, unlikely to say, 'Mum, play with me.' So, this is a golden time to spend quality time with your child (especially when he is young) to understand him well, his values, his passions, and so on.

- **Self-acceptance**

Teach children to accept themselves as they are. If they're not good at maths, then that's OK. Teach them that it's impossible for one person to excel at everything. For instance, M.S. Dhoni is a great cricketer, but he's not a great painter. Encourage children to accept themselves as they are. It fosters self-acceptance, and in the future, they will likely avoid comparing themselves with others. This way, children can understand their inner strengths, interests, dislikes, and likes. When things are not working or are causing stress, teach them that it's OK to walk away. It's fine to quit and start a new hobby with excitement.

It doesn't matter whether a passion is big or small. Children put their heart into their passion, though they may change it later. When children follow their passion, they live in the moment. They feel free to be themselves. No stress can touch them when they're fully immersed in something they love. In one word, they feel happy.

So, go ahead and support your child's passion. Don't burn them out, don't exhaust them, and don't criticise them. Consider a child's life to be as crystal clear as our vision through properly cleaned glass. There is no right or wrong in the choice of passion. Leave worry behind.

Now, it's time to wear a clean pair of glasses and move on to the next chapter.

Chapter 4

Childhood Stress

"Stress" is a very common word that we often use. After returning home from the office, a husband says, 'The day was too stressful.' A young child says, 'I am stressed about my upcoming exam.' A tired wife says, 'I'm stressed about how I can finish all the dishes within 3 hours for the party,' etc. So first, let's discuss what stress is.

Stress is a feeling of worry or mental tension caused by different situations around us. A small amount of stress is not harmful at all. For instance, a racing heartbeat before entering the dentist's room, before performing on stage, or before giving a speech are examples of harmless stress. Both adults and children can handle this type of stress. But when stress lasts for a long time, it damages both our mental and physical health. In one sentence, when we fail to handle stress, it has an adverse effect on our lives.

When the human body experiences stress, stress hormones—mainly cortisol and adrenaline—are secreted. Cortisol is the primary stress hormone, which increases blood sugar. These hormones help us deal with stressful situations by increasing heart rate, blood pressure, and glucose uptake in the brain, reducing inflammation, causing muscle weakness, weight gain, and so on.

So, it is our responsibility to teach our children to cope with stress. Children are not born with the skill to handle stress; they learn gradually with the help of their parents and experiences. It is not possible to avoid stress entirely, but it is possible to reduce stress levels. Physical symptoms caused by stress are often misunderstood and overlooked. We might take medicine to soothe our bodies (which can be necessary) but ignore and refuse to investigate the true cause. Stress can lead to depression, anxiety, trembling hands, and sometimes hallucinations. Therefore, all of us, including our children, should aim to stay away from stress. As I mentioned, children do not come equipped with the skill to handle stress efficiently, so parental intervention is needed. However, if parents are overly concerned about stress and intervene too often, this can also be harmful. Allow children to manage some stress by themselves so they can become more self-reliant.

Hans Selye introduced the concept of 2 types of stress: "Eustress" and "Distress." "Eustress" has a positive effect on the human body, while "Distress" negatively affects on physical and mental health. According to research, there are mainly 3 types of stress: (i) Acute Stress, (ii) Episodic Stress, and (iii) Chronic Stress.

I. Acute Stress

This is the most common form of stress and lasts for a very short time. It appears suddenly and produces a "fight-or-flight" response in our bodies. It occurs in children when they are suddenly exposed to loud sounds, danger, fear of isolation, crowding, attending a new activity, going to a new school, etc.

II. Episodic Stress

When acute stress is experienced too frequently, it is called "episodic stress." This is observed in children who are highly competitive in nature and have high expectations of themselves. When children have unrealistic or unreasonable demands, they often suffer from episodic stress. It generally lasts a few days or up to a month.

III. Chronic Stress

Chronic stress exists for a long duration, and the individual cannot get sufficient time to relax and continues to feel pressure. It often causes serious health problems (sweating hands, nightmares, fast heart rate) and mental problems (lack of concentration, short-term memory loss, difficulty in adapting new things, and so on). Children experience chronic stress when they lose a parent, lose someone close to them, face abuse, endure sexual harassment, deal with family financial problems, experience separation between parents, face an unfriendly school environment, or feel deprived due to a newborn in the family, and so on.

Among the above-mentioned types of stress, some are manageable and give a push to try new things or encourage children to attempt a new activity. This is known as positive stress or eustress, as mentioned before. However, events like losing someone, divorce, or the arrival of a new baby are examples of tolerable stress that children can handle with proper love and care. Sexual harassment, abuse, and neglect are examples of toxic stress that children cannot easily handle. If left untreated, toxic stress has a very negative impact on brain development. It can affect not only brain development but also cause malfunctioning of various organs.

To protect our children, it is necessary to understand the causes of stress, recognise the symptoms of stress, and learn how to manage these effectively to achieve a better childhood for them. Let's take a look at the causes of childhood stress.

Causes of Childhood Stress

- **Loud Sound**

Toddlers often cry when they are exposed to loud sounds. Our auditory system identifies the intensity of sound and creates a stress response in the body as a "fight-or-flight" reaction.

- **Separation**

When a toddler or preschooler is separated from his parents or caregiver, stress is generated. This is why toddlers or preschoolers often cry on their first day at crèche or school. Separation places them in unfamiliar situations, and they do not yet know how to cope with it. Sometimes, even a teenager separated from home for higher studies experiences stress hormones in his body, though this stress does not last long.

- **Strangers**

In some countries, there are many examples of crimes where children are kidnapped and sold. To protect children, parents naturally warn them not to talk to strangers, as they may kidnap them or steal valuable things from them. As a result, when children see a stranger, they refuse to interact, and a small amount of stress hormone is released in their bodies. When a toddler sees a stranger, it is similar to the feeling an adult might have when seeing a tiger in front of him, triggering the body's "fight-or-flight" response.

- **School**

If the school environment is not healthy, it causes stress among children. A good school environment includes low noise levels, cleanliness, airy rooms, sufficient water, clean and hygienic toilets and latrines, the absence of overcrowding, and friendly teachers and staff. If one or 2 of these are missing, it can cause stress among children. If teachers are too strict, angry, and often shout at children, some children may simply refuse to go to school. Soon, school becomes a place of punishment for them. They might often tell you that they have a stomach ache or headache. In this case, parental intervention is necessary, as this type of stress appears daily, resembling episodic stress. If ignored, it can may turn into chronic stress.

- **Pressure of Homework**

Constant worry about completing homework and assignments on time creates stress among children. Sometimes, parents also create pressure to study hard, resulting in a lack of free time for play. Continuous pressure to finish homework often has a negative impact on cognitive function, emotional regulation, and sleep. Overall, excessive pressure to complete homework reduces the free time that children need for themselves, leading to issues like anxiety, depression, poor digestion, hormonal imbalance, and poor concentration.

- **Fear of Ghosts and the Dark**

Parents and caregivers often use stories about ghosts or give misconceptions about the dark to scare children so that, they won't go outside while the caregivers are resting. Their intention is to protect children, ensuring they don't go outside alone at night or during the day without permission. However, this can have a negative effect on children's minds. Children begin to imagine terrifying ghostly faces, they fear and gradually this fear overtakes them. They may refuse to sleep alone, and as a result, this fear creates stress, increasing cortisol and adrenaline levels in the body. Exposure to horrifying and scary videos can also trigger stress in the body, sometimes leading to panic attacks due to ghost-related imagination.

I remember an incident from my own early childhood. My mum used to say that if you went outside alone at noon or in the afternoon, a ghost would throw stones at you, and when you tried to see it, there would be no one there. This scared me, and I never tried to go outside, allowing my mum to take her nap. But the fear was so strong that I refused to go alone to my neighbour's house to play with my friend. My mum had to drop me off there, even though it was right next door. She scolded me but forgot the reason I was doing so. The cause is the fear, she instilled in me. So, don't create panic in children; it is harmful to their growth.

- **Doctor and Vaccine**

Medical treatment is always painful. Vaccination is a must, and it is a nightmare for some children, as nightmares create stress. Once, my son had a toothache, so I made an appointment with a dentist. The dentist told me that there was a swelling in his gum and cut the gum to release it. My son experienced severe pain during this process. After 3 months, when I booked another appointment for a regular check-up, my son began to show his anxiety upon learning about another visit to the dentist. At that moment, cortisol and adrenaline were at peak levels in his body.

- **News of Natural Disasters and Accidents**

Natural disasters like tsunamis, earthquakes, cyclones, and tornadoes threaten humankind. Many people lose their lives, homes, and loved ones. When we watch such news on television, we must remember that our little one is at home and he is also watching this. Such life-taking disasters often create panic among young children. They fear losing their lives, parents, or homes as depicted on television. As a result, stress hormones increase in their bodies. Children can experience trauma when they see bodies buried under debris on television or if they have witnessed an accident. This stress and trauma can be exacerbated by their parents' stress, and this may cause serious physical or mental health problems among children. If a family faces an accident or a disaster, children in that family may suffer from serious physical and mental problems, which can last far longer than we might think.

- **Engagement in More Than One Activity**

Too many burdens often cause stress among children. Sometimes they become rebellious, showing tantrums, but parents fail to understand why. As a result, stress overtakes their minds and bodies, gradually turning into chronic stress. Parents engage their children in more than one activity, like drawing, cricket, dancing, singing, and so on, and children become exhausted, as described in the chapter "Find and Nurture Passion." There is no free time for children. Children are always busy to satisfy parent's need and desire by worsening their mental and physical conditions. Yes, it is the stress hormones that soon take the responsibility of their bodies.

- **Fear of Making Friends or Peer Problems**

Making friends and maintaining friendships requires skills. It is taught in pre-school. These skills involve sharing, talking politely to others, waiting for one's turn, helping each other, cooperating, listening to others, and sorting out disagreements with others. Sometimes, we as parents have to intervene to sort out peer problems. Children who are introverted and suffer from social anxiety disorder face challenges in making friends, causing stress. Social anxiety disorder is an intense feeling of being watched or judged by others, accompanied by negative thoughts and beliefs about oneself. This fear creates a boundary, preventing children from opening up or expressing their true feelings. They suppress their true feelings, which generates stress.

When a child faces difficulty in making friends and becomes depressed from loneliness, cortisol and adrenaline hormones take control of his body.

It is not always true that our children cannot make friends. Sometimes their peers simply refuse to make friendships with them or deny playing with them. My son faced such a problem. He is harmonious and affable and became more adaptable as he grew up. He always wanted to go out and loved to have fun with his friends. But one day, when he heard about a party we were going to attend with his pre-school friend's family, named Shourya, he began to cry and refused to attend that party. After a discussion, I learned that there had been issues at the last 2 parties that we had attended with my son's friend's family and another family who were friends with my son's friend's mother.

Yes, I knew there were problems between my son and Shourya and his mother's friend's daughter, Rosy. I simply ignored it and thought, like other parents, that it was my son's problem to adjust with his friends. So, I again forced him to attend the third party, and my son became rebellious. Then I decided to attend that party for the last time to find out the real problem. Yes, I know I made a mistake. But, believe me, I just wanted to find the actual cause of the problem. Eventually, the day of the third party arrived. We joined the party. I silently observed the children. Soon, I realised it was not my son's problem. Rosy and Shourya made a plan, hit my son, and played a game unfamiliar to him, telling him, 'You cannot play as you do not know this game.' Both Shourya and Rosy continued playing, leaving my son alone. Such situations definitely create stress not only among young children but also adults. I wanted to help my son socialise, as we lived far from our home and relatives, and this was the only reason for arranging parties.

So, it is not always as we believe. It is not always our or our children's fault. Be careful to protect your child from stress. Yes, after this incident, I never arranged or joined any parties with Rosy and Shourya again. I just wanted to stop the cortisol and adrenaline hormones released in my son's body during those parties.

- **Bullying**

Bullying occurs when someone more powerful and aggressive targets another. Bullying includes physical violence like hitting, striking, kicking, intentionally tripping, spitting on someone, etc. Verbal bullying includes teasing, threatening physical harm ('I will see you; come here; I will kill you'), name-calling with offensive language, yelling, using abusive language, spreading rumours about someone, intentionally excluding someone from an activity, gossiping, etc. Naturally, if anyone—be it an adult or a child—goes through such bullying, their mental and physical health are at risk. It has adverse effects that sometimes become uncontrollable. Bullying impairs the social development of both children and adults.

Bullying is enough to destroy a child's life. Children can be victimised in school, on the playground, and in other professional classes. Children who are bullied are more likely to suffer from depression, anxiety, sadness, loneliness, loss of interest in things they once enjoyed, and changes in sleeping and eating patterns. These effects can even persist into adulthood if not treated properly. It is often observed that there is a link between suicide and bullying. Although bullying is not the sole cause of suicide, depression, anxiety, and loneliness also contribute to suicidal tendencies among young children. Yes, children are at risk. Therefore, it is not only our responsibility but also that of society to eliminate bullying.

Children who bully others are also at risk. In adulthood, they are more likely to become addicted to alcohol, tobacco, and drugs. They often engage in fights, destroy others' property, and may even drop out of school. They may abuse their partners, children, or even their parents. In short, their lives become meaningless. So, both the children who bully and those who are bullied are in danger. It is our duty to protect them and foster a healthier society. Nowadays, bullying is strictly prohibited in schools and colleges. To control it, there are punishments enforced by school and college authorities. Hopefully, we will soon achieve a bullying-free world. It is often difficult for teachers or parents to recognise whether a child is a victim of bullying, as it usually happens out of sight. Remember the incident I mentioned with Shourya and Rosy at the party. So, if our child continuously refuses to go to school or attend parties, there is a possibility of bullying. Of course, there may be other reasons for such behaviour, so parents need to observe carefully to find the actual cause and intervene immediately to protect their children, as they are often unable to deal with it alone.

- **Change of Residence and School**

If parents have a transferable job, children may have to change their residence and school as well. Adjusting to a new home or school can be very frustrating for children, generating stress. Children miss their friends and their old home so much that it takes a lot of time for them to recover from this trauma. They feel stress in making new friends and in adapting to the school environment. Frequent changes in residence or school may lead to poor social development in children. Depression, anxiety, sleepless nights, poor digestion, etc., are often side effects of this stress.

- **Fear of Rejection**

Children who are continuously rejected by their parents, teachers, or peers have a tendency to develop a "fear of rejection." We can consider "fear of rejection" as part of "social anxiety." According to research, children who have been abused during their formative years may develop complex post-traumatic stress disorder (CPTSD), which may cause "fear of rejection." Besides that, some children who are continuously seeking validation from others, are shy, sensitive to criticism, or overly perfectionistic, often suffer from "fear of rejection." Well, we all have to face rejection to some extent. But a child has a more adverse effect than an adult. This may hamper the development of a child, and the generated stress creates lots of problems like difficulty in making good relationships, poor communication skills, difficulty in making eye contact, adopting rigid postures, avoiding parties or other social gatherings, difficulty in group work, and so on. So, "fear of rejection" should be treated immediately in childhood for better adulthood.

- **Blackmail**

Basically, it starts with the help of a parent. Some parents tend to blackmail children by saying, 'If you don't do this, I will complain to your teacher," who may have scolded them before. In panic, children start to do what their parents advise or request. These types of children grow up in an abnormal domestic environment. These children are definitely under stress, but the worst effect is seen when these types of children start to blackmail their peers to satisfy their intentions. Basically, these children target calm and introverted children. As a result, both the children who blackmail and those who are blackmailed are under stress, but those who are blackmailed in school or college are in more danger.

- **Financial Problem**

When parents suffer from financial loss, anxiety strikes them. Some children are so sensitive that they can pick up the emotions of their depressed parents with ease. When younger children become aware of their family's financial problems due to business loss or job loss, they are at a high-stress level. They start to blame themselves for the financial loss. They feel distress or stress when they fail to join any school trip due to a financial crisis or are unable to take good food to school. They alone cannot handle such stress. Stress engulfs them. So, they often suffer from sleepless nights, stomach aches, headaches, poor concentration, unfriendly relationships with others, and so on. Continuous worry about the future also makes them ill. Parents communicate with their children in a tense voice or short temper; soon children develop negative emotions. Children lose self-esteem, attach to negative peer groups, and engage in delinquency. In this case, parental support is necessary. Yes, it is hard to achieve serenity when you are thrown into hardship. But positive parenting practice is needed to nurture children. Instead of being distressed, search for a positive solution that works better for your family. Suppose you may stop yoga classes to save extra money and practise it at home. This not only helps you to maintain a good life but also sends positive feedback to your little one on how to stay positive in bleak situations.

- **Insulting a Child in Front of Others or Using Offensive Language**

Imagine your boss insults you in front of your colleagues. Now tell me, how do you feel? Is this OK, or does it feel humiliating? I know everyone has prestige and being humiliated makes anyone upset, angry, and lose self-esteem. The same happens to our little ones if we scold them in front of others. Childhood is full of mistakes, and we have to correct them patiently. If we scold our children in front of their friends, relatives, or strangers, or use offensive language, they easily get hurt emotionally and become upset or even lose their self-esteem. Naturally, they feel stress when they are with us, constantly wondering, 'Is this the right thing I've done? If I do something wrong, Mum will scold me.' If other caregivers like teachers or grandparents do the same, children easily lose hope and self-confidence. Soon, children withdraw their attention from activities they loved. They may simply refuse to go to school or deny playing in groups where conflicts might arise. Besides that, they may start telling lies to avoid humiliation. I have already faced such problems. When my son was 6 years old, I took him to a cricket academy just for some physical exercise—nothing more than that. The academy allowed it, but there was a teacher whose behaviour was too harsh towards my child. He used to abuse my son physically and mentally. His stress hormones increased. Soon he lost his interest in cricket and left the academy forever. So, harsh words and rude behaviour are enough to kill a child's self-confidence. If parents and other caregivers continue to use offensive language and insult children often, they are effectively killing the souls of those children. In the film *Taare Zameen Par*, Aamir Khan mentions that in the Solomon Islands, the tribes don't cut down a tree. They surround the tree and curse it for hours every day, and within a few weeks, the tree dries up and dies.

- **Quarrelling Parents**

Stress hormones affect children when parents are quarrelling. Believe it or not, children pick up on just about everything. The stress from yelling parents is easily absorbed by little ones, even when they appear busy playing with their favourite toys. Children simply pick up on the stress levels at home, school, or anywhere they go. They don't understand what triggers them, but they absorb stress and act accordingly. So, stressed parents create a stressed child. A stressed child either becomes very quiet or exhibits harsh behaviour, mirroring what he has observed during his parents' quarrels.

- **Extensive Screen Time**

When we spend several hours on our mobile devices, we feel exhausted and irritable. The same happens to our little ones when we allow them to spend a lot of time with electronic devices (mobile, computer, or television). Let's explore how and why extensive screen time creates stress among children.

- Light emitted from digital screens disrupts our sleep cycle. Melatonin is high in our body at night. Light coming from screens gives a signal of daytime to our body, and our body suppresses the production of melatonin. The body delays the release of melatonin, and hence the sleep cycle is hampered. So, before going to bed, if we allow extensive screen time, it will definitely hamper the sleep cycle of our children.

- When children enjoy video games, cartoons, films, or shorts, the happy hormone dopamine is secreted. Too much dopamine reduces focus. Suppose a child enjoys his game too much, so he simply ignores his daily homework or study. But at the time of exams, he will find himself helpless. So, too much screen time relates to enjoyment, which increases high dopamine levels in our body, and as a result, we shift our focus from crucial tasks.

- When children have too much screen time, they deny performing any outdoor activity. Outdoor activities like walking, running, cycling, swimming, and so on are helpful for our body and also increase our brain capacity. When children exercise, blood flow increases, allowing more brain cells to get more nutrients from blood. According to John Medina, in his book *Brain Rules*, he describes:

Outdoor physical activity stimulates the brain's most powerful factor, BDNF (Brain-Derived Neurotrophic Factor), which helps in the development of healthy brain tissue and encourages neurogenesis (formation of new brain cells). BDNF thrives in the hippocampus area, which is responsible for memory formation.

So, to improve memory, better the learning process, and enhance cognitive functions, we should cut down screen time and expose our children to outdoor activities.

- **Divorce**

Like quarrelling parents, separation between father and mother can also create stress among children. A child needs to stay with both mum and dad for proper mental and physical growth. He deserves a good, healthy home environment on which his mental and physical growth is completely dependent. But an unhappy marriage ends in divorce, which creates cortisol and adrenaline in the couple's body as well as in their children's bodies.

I know a boy who lives with his mum, who has just separated from her husband and is going through a financial crisis. As we know, financial crisis hits the stress button in a child's body. So, that boy suffers from stress and becomes a depressed kid. After getting divorced, when one or both parents engage in a new relationship, this is also too hard for young children to accept. Soon, stress spreads into children's bodies and minds. Children cannot handle such pressure and soon trap themselves in a web of depression and anxiety. They often fall sick. In adulthood, some children simply deny getting involved in relationships. Children's self-esteem drops. They have to adjust in schools, colleges, and society. They have to compromise on their careers. They start to hate either one or both parents or start to hate themselves. And the worst effect is when teenagers commit suicide or get involved in crime.

- **Sibling Rivalry**

Sibling rivalry is common in a family with more than one child. It is the jealousy, competition, and fighting between children. Mainly, sibling rivalry arises when a second child joins the family. Before the newborn baby, the elder one gets all the attention from the parents. But with the second baby, the elder one suddenly starts to feel that he does not get as much attention as he did before. The elder one thinks that he has to compete with his sibling to get his parents' attention and love. And to some extent, it is true. Parents get busy taking care of the newborn baby, and naturally, time for the elder one is reduced, which generates stress for the elder child. The elder child becomes angry with the parents, starts to disobey them, and ignores the advice given to him. Irritation, misbehaviour, shouting, and ignoring are common among such children (mainly the elder ones). It is very frustrating for parents. Such children start to hate their siblings. They irritate them, snatch toys, do not listen to others, or do the opposite of what they are told. When parents continuously compare them with their siblings, the situation becomes worse. In this case, sibling rivalry can also exist even when siblings are not related by blood. Children can feel like they are in competition with their step-sibling, biological sibling, or adopted sibling.

Though sibling rivalry starts in childhood, it has a tendency to continue into adulthood. Here are some causes that may create sibling rivalry:

- Unequal attention distribution by parents.

- When one child feels he was treated differently from his sibling.

- When parents give preference to one child, naturally, the other thinks it is unfair, and frustration strikes him.

- Comparison by parents between siblings makes the situation worse. In this case, parents should believe that each child is different and unique.

- When children grow, if one (maybe elder or younger) develops more skills and talents than the other, then the other child may feel threatened or embarrassed. This can lead to unnecessary competition and aggression.

- When parents give all the responsibilities to one child, the other thinks he is not capable and suffers from either depression and low self-esteem or becomes aggressive or revengeful.

Sibling rivalry is stressful for both parents and children. Leaving it untreated may spoil a child's life and lead the child to engage in revengeful actions. I know of a brother and his elder sister who locked her little three-year-old brother in a closet. After some time, their mother asked her about her brother, and she told her she had locked him in. Luckily, the boy was saved by his mother. The little girl was only 5 years old. Later, I heard that girl was actually treated very badly. Her brother was a calmer child, whereas that girl was noisy in that family. Getting less attention from her mother, that girl felt abandoned. To get attention from her mother, she never missed a chance to do mischievous tasks.

- **Population**

Earth is the only planet where life exists. On this earth, only 29% is covered with land, soil, and natural resources. So, the land where we live is constant, and our natural resources like petrol, coal, and plants on earth are also in a fixed amount. For civilisation, the first humans started to cut down trees and use natural resources for the benefit of mankind.

In the early stages of civilisation, we accessed resources freely, but now we have to pay for them. As the population increases day by day, humans have to compete with each other to access resources, which remain constant. Those who pay more are able to access resources and other commodities in modern society. Due to the population in city areas, we can see high-rise buildings where approximately 100 to 300 or more people live together. Naturally, for one vacant post (job), there are lakhs of applicants. For people nowadays, the main motto is to survive in this competitive world. As we approach the future, earth becomes a tougher place to survive. For this reason, parents feel stressed about the future of their children. They sometimes, subconsciously or consciously, create pressure on their children. They just want to secure their children's lives. Naturally, our modern world creates stressed children who are the backbone of the nation. Due to this uncontrolled population, childhood is in danger.

Symptoms of Stress

When children fail to handle stress, various anxiety symptoms are generated within them. These may be either physical or emotional. Sometimes these symptoms are so subtle that we take them lightly and refuse to intervene. The earlier you help your child, the sooner he returns from an anxious state to happiness. To understand whether your child is under stress, here are some common behavioural signs, which include:

- Excessive worry about everything
- Behavioural changes like moodiness, aggressiveness, short temper
- Crying more frequently
- Clinging to caregivers more than usual
- Irritability
- Becoming more demanding
- Restlessness
- Poor concentration and memory
- Developing fear about separation
- School refusal
- Avoiding family parties or social gatherings
- Avoiding meeting new people
- Hesitating to start conversations
- Refusing to make new friends
- Avoiding group activity
- Fear of losing control
- Excessive worry about being negatively judged
- Avoiding answering in class, oral exams, and reading aloud
- Experiencing loneliness
- Developing habits like nail-biting, lip-biting, or sucking fingers
- Teenagers may have a tendency to become alcoholic
- Unable to control emotions
- Stubborn behaviour

- Few peer friendships outside the family
- Worry about the future
- Explosive and loud

Some physical symptoms that arise during stress are

- Headache
- Stomachache
- Decreased appetite or changes in eating habits
- Eating frequently or overeating
- Bedwetting
- Nightmares
- Sleep disturbance
- Poor digestion or upset stomach
- Shortness of breath
- Dizziness
- Excessive sweating
- Heart palpitations
- Muscle tension
- Exhaustion
- Tight chest
- Other physical symptoms with no physical illness

How Parents Can Help

Parents can help children reduce their stress in healthy ways. Here are some steps:

- Provide a safe, secure, friendly environment at home.
- Ensure a non-hectic family routine.

- Spend quality time with children.

- Plan outings or have dinner together.

- Avoid watching news about floods, earthquakes, landslides, and other life-threatening natural disasters in front of children.

- News about car crashes, wars, and train accidents should also be avoided in front of children.

- Plan some physical exercise.

- Reduce screen time for both you and your child.

- Be patient and listen to your child carefully; otherwise, he may not discuss his problems with you in the future. If he is in trouble, he may not tell you due to ignorance, which could lead to danger.

- Avoid responding too quickly after hearing something from your child or when he has done something wrong.

- Do not offer suggestions too often when your child talks about a problem. Let them handle situations themselves or discuss them. This helps children gain confidence in themselves.

- Do not scold children in front of others.

- Scrutinise content before allowing your child to watch any videos. Negative videos, such as those featuring monsters, ghosts, violence, or adult content, should be prohibited, as these can create stress.

- Be a role model. Children follow you, so choose your words wisely and try to stay calm in stressful moments. Manage your stress in a healthy way.

- If your child fails to perform in any show or game, don't criticise him. Help boost his mood. Your positive words are the strength of your little one. Teach him to forget what has happened and help him look forward to new hopes. This will help your little one handle stressful situations.

- Don't compare your child with peers or others.

- Build your child's sense of self-worth. Use encouragement, love, and affection.

- Assign easy activities that lead to success.

- Allow children to make some decisions so they feel they are not worthless.

- Don't discuss your financial problems in front of your child.

- Love your child as he is. Avoid a mindset of "others can do it, and you cannot." This will help your child learn to accept himself, which is essential to becoming a happy person later in life.

- If you have more than one child, try to make fair decisions. Don't give any one child special treatment.

- Engage in fewer activities and allow some spare time (without digital screens).

- Do yoga with children. Yoga helps reduce stress.

- Teach children deep-breathing exercises or mindfulness, which are also helpful for reducing stress.

- Tell stories or read books to help your child learn how characters in stories deal with anxiety.

- Encourage children to write down their feelings. This is a simple way to deal with anxiety. For example, writing about positive things they are grateful for reduces stress levels, while writing about negative things that upset them helps them understand their internal feelings. This can help them cope with their stress.

- Always talk politely with children. A loud voice creates stress.

- Recognise unsolved stress symptoms in children.

Parents need to consult a therapist, counsellor, or paediatrician if a child continues to withdraw, becomes more unhappy or depressed, has problems in school or interacting with friends, or is unable to control anger.

Children will be happy if they learn how to cope with stress and anxiety. Happy children are not free from anxiety, but they simply know how to handle stress to return to their happy state as soon as possible.

Chapter 5

Tantrums and Children

Once I visited a mall, where a little girl, about 5 years old, came with her parents for shopping. She wanted to buy a big chocolate, but her parents refused. When refused, she suddenly outburst in rage, cried, shouted, even lay on the floor with her eyes closed, screaming. To control the embarrassing situation, her parents soon bought the chocolate for her. She then stopped showing rage. This is an example of a tantrum.

Tantrums are common in childhood. A tantrum is a strong emotional expression that occurs due to unmet wants or desires. When a child does not get what she wants or is unable to make someone do what she wants, she bursts into anger or frustration. Sometimes, tantrums can happen when a child is tired, hungry, suffers from a lack of sleep, or experiences other physical discomfort. A child may show irritation when wearing uncomfortable clothing with rough fabrics or tags. It is our duty to evaluate the actual cause behind the tantrum. Mainly, children between 1 to 4 years old show tantrums, though sometimes this may continue for an additional 2 years. Toddlers who cannot express their feelings or needs well have a strong tendency to show tantrums. This is because, between 1 and 3 years of age, toddlers are learning language, which is complicated. This leads to frustration, and they may burst into anger. As language skills improve, tantrums tend to decrease.

Signs that a child is in frustration include:

- Crying

- Screaming and yelling

- Throwing things

- Hurting themselves

- Hurting others

- Stamping

- Kicking

- Biting

- Throwing themselves on the floor

- Deliberately not eating

Causes of Tantrums

Here are some causes that create tantrums among children. If we are aware of these, we can soothe them during a tantrum or simply avoid its occurrence. These causes include:

- Lack of sleep

- Exhaustion

- Hunger

- Not getting what they want, like chocolates, toys, pens, etc.

- Wanting attention from parents

- When someone refuses to do what they want

- Being given foods they strongly dislike

- Wearing clothes with hard, itchy, and uncomfortable fabrics

- Wearing clothes with tags or stickers

- Toys being broken by others

- Toys being snatched by a sibling or other children

- Being told to do tasks they have refused

- Other physical problems (e.g., stomachache, leg pain, etc.) that require medical attention

There are different types of character among children; some are extroverts, some are introverts, and some lie in between these 2 characteristics. When you raise a child who is extroverted, they have a tendency to show tantrums more often than an introverted one. Mainly, high-intensity children are more prone to show tantrums. They just shout to get what they need or want to do. High-intensity children become exhausted when a tantrum attacks them. Shouting, crying, and stamping do not help them to feel good; they do that to seek help from their caregivers. Yes, I know they are loud, but they are struggling with their strong emotions (anger, frustration, and disappointment). Another unfortunate aspect is that high-intensity children get different negative comments from their parents and siblings. Parents do this because they feel they can't control them. Siblings do it out of jealousy, as high-intensity children get more attention from their parents.

Children who externalise their emotions have a tendency to react first and think later. They do things without considering the consequences. So, when they calm down, they feel guilty. At this point, they feel helpless and seek help from their parents.

On the other hand, children who internalise their emotions struggle to express their feelings properly when they are frustrated. These children also need special treatment to channel their feelings. A question-and-answer process is the best way to help them. Ask them, 'What happened?', 'Why are you upset?', 'Is everything OK?', and soon you will get the answer 'No, I am not,' along with the reason why. Then, by discussing their feelings and exploring how to deal with them, you can help your child manage frustration.

Running away from frustration is not the best way to deal with it. First, help your child acknowledge frustration, then teach him how to deal with it positively. When a child has a tantrum and parents remain calm and focused, the child will learn that anger is acceptable but should be handled in a calm, natural way. Tantrums are natural feelings that can happen at any time. We cannot avoid tantrums, but by taking small steps, we can easily minimise their frequency and intensity.

Here Are Some Steps to Tame Tantrums

- Provide food on time, so that your little one does not suffer from hunger.

- Try not to disrupt their daily routine.

- Ensure an adequate amount of sleep. Mainly, toddlers (1-3 years old) need 11 to 14 hours of sleep, preschoolers (3 to 5 years old) need 10 to 13 hours, school-aged children (5 to 12 years old) need 9 to 12 hours, and teenagers (13 to 18 years old) need 8 to 10 hours.

- Ensure sufficient time for relaxation.

- Avoid engaging them in more than one activity that could cause exhaustion.

- Mainly toddlers should be provided with soft, cotton clothes without tags.

- Ask for their preference, like 'What do you like to eat, banana or mango?' 'What would you like to buy, a frock or a skirt?', and so on. By doing this, you ensure they feel they can make their own decisions. It gives children a sense of control over themselves.

- Ensure they have a place at home where they can sit alone to internalise their feelings when they are upset or in extreme anger. This place is known as a "safe place" where a child can feel secure while processing his anger.

- Children who have a tendency to harm themselves need monitoring by parents when they are told to sit alone in the "safe place" at home. Always stay nearby, so they cannot harm themselves or others.

- Be calm and focused when a tantrum hits your child. Your calmness sends a signal to your child that anger can be controlled in a positive way.

- Distract children when they start to show initial signs of a tantrum.

- Provide soothing music and light which help to keep them calm.

- Provide light-shaded clothes, as colour can impact a child's mood, just like it does ours. Soothing-coloured walls are also helpful in reducing the intensity of tantrums.

- Gently and calmly persuade your child when he demands a toy and you do not agree to buy it.

- Sometimes it is better to ignore tantrums that are intentionally created by your children. If they understand that tantrums have no effect on their parents, they will stop showing intentionally created tantrums.

- Request the host to keep all desired items out of reach from children when you visit someone's house.

- Engage them in activities that are easy for them to succeed in.

- Parents should play board games like chess, Ludo, and Snakes and Ladders. These games help children to concentrate on the present situation and increase their frustration tolerance. Any board game involves turn-taking, waiting, a bit of luck, and controlling emotions when losing a game. When a child loses, he may bursts into anger, and when he wins, he may dance. Sometimes, it is necessary for children to lose, so that you can teach them how to control emotional outbursts positively by telling them that losing is normal, and they can win next time.

- If you allow the child to win every time, then you miss the opportunity to teach him how to control a tantrum. I used this board game technique to tame the frustrations in my son's mind. Sometimes I allow my son to win and sometimes to lose. Every child wants to win, which gives them confidence, but losing leaves them emotionally overwhelmed. So, naturally, when my son lost, he became emotionally overwhelmed, and it was the right moment I was waiting for. I told him, 'Situations and conditions will not always be favourable. We have to accept such situations and should act accordingly. If you cry, you don't win. It is better to try again and identify what mistake led you to lose the game. Let's learn from mistakes, improve yourself, and perform better than before.' I also used to say, 'It is a continuous process. As long as we live, we learn. Learning from our mistakes is a good habit, which helps us to move forward in life. Don't lose hope.'

- Give a hug to control a tantrum. Yes, physical comfort melts anger like extinguishing a fire by pouring water. I often use it, and you should try it. It is actually the *Jaddu ki Jhappi in Munna Bhai MBBS*. It has a magical power. Anytime you feel your child is not OK, just use this *Jaddu ki Jhappi*.

What You Will Do When Child Has a Tantrum

Parents become frustrated when children show tantrums. They first try to control tantrums, but, failing sometimes, they shout at the children. This frustrating cycle continues until children learn to deal with tantrums. However, shouting and scolding may have a reverse effect on children. Children learn to shout or show frustration more intensely than before. So, it is better to hold your emotions. Inspired by you, your child can understand that by keeping oneself calm and cool, one can handle tough situations. If you are the parent of a high-intensity child, then patience is a must. You should practise breathing exercises with your child to keep yourself in control.

When a tantrum strikes, give children some time to cool down. If tantrums occur in a public place, some parents quickly buy the toy or chocolates the child demands. However, by doing so, parents encourage children to have tantrums in public places. This time, try not to buy anything to calm them down. Quickly leave that place with your children. Go somewhere else, give them some time to calm down, then give them a hug and politely tell them that their behaviour are not acceptable. Lastly, distract them and engage them in a new activity, like giving a ride on a toy train, enjoying a pizza together, and so on.

When children burst out in anger at home and completely refuse to listen to their parents, send them to the "safe place," and gradually you will see their anger decrease.

When children control their anger, appreciate them and give them a small reward, like making their favourite food, going on a shopping trip, taking them to the park, playing with them, and so on. Your appreciation gives your child the strength to control his anger in the future.

It is better for a tantrum-prone child to take 4 deep breaths first before being asked what has happened. This helps the child control himself. Lastly, discuss the problems that made him upset.

If you plan to buy a toy that is highly desired by your child and for which he cried and shouted, try not to buy the toy at the moment of the tantrum. Give it later and make sure he understands that he got it because he tried to control his tantrum, not because he showed his anger.

In this regard, I want to share a story about how my son learned to control his tantrums. My son was a high-intensity child, but by the age of 7, he could control his anger. One day, at his friend's birthday party, we bought 2 nice yellow smiley-designed pens for both him and his friend. He just loved it. He played with that pen all day long. By the evening, he found a crack that he had made in his pen, and he showed anger, cried, and demanded to give the broken pen to his friend.

So that he could take the undamaged pen, which was already wrapped. We tried hard to control his anger, but we failed. Time was ticking; we were already late for the party. The phone rang, asking when we would join the party. It was one of the most frustrating and embarrassing moments I have ever faced. Suddenly, my husband, usually a calm person. He gave him a light smack on the leg (of course, the intensity was low). After this, my son was shocked and stopped crying. He was surprised, as he had never received such behaviour from his father before. Then my husband calmly told him, 'Do you know who is smiling now?'

My son was speechless. Then my husband continued, 'Your anger sitting inside your mind is smiling. Your anger thinks, Yes, it is so much fun, and I am successful in my work because Reyansh got a smack. He he...' My husband also explained that 'anger is a monster. It always tries to harm us. It is our duty to control the anger monster to keep us safe.' From that day, my little son, Reyansh, learned how to control his anger. Now, when he is angry, he simply goes into his room (his safe place), cries, and tries to control his "anger monster." A few moments later, he comes out of the room and tells us, 'Look, I can control anger. Anger cannot control me.' We smile and give him a hug and lots of appreciation.

It is true that we cannot remove frustrations from our lives, but we can change our response to them.

Children Should Practise

One cannot control themselves if they do not want to. Yes, this is also true for our children. But to understand such a philosophy, they are not yet mature enough. So, it is our duty to teach children to follow some steps when they feel anger or frustration.

Here are some steps:

- **Story of the anger monster**

Tell your children, when they are angry, that the "anger monster" comes and takes control of their lives. As I mentioned already, my husband was able to help my son control his anger by telling him that "anger is a monster." You should also tell your children that this monster does all the wrong things through them and that, in the end, the children will suffer in pain while the monster laughs. So, tell children to practise talking to themselves when they are angry, saying, 'Anger is a monster. It cannot control my life. I can control it. Just leave.' By practising this, their brains also start to believe that they can control anger, and gradually, you will see the results.

- **Make a mad list**

Tell your children to make a list of things that make them mad. Help them make the list so they do not feel lonely. Next, after completing the list, read it aloud. Finally, tear up the list, make a ball with it, and kick it out of the house – symbolically out of their minds. This exercise provides physical relief and makes children laugh. Through this list, both children and parents come to understand the actual causes that create frustrations, which later convert into tantrums.

- **Kicking anger emoji**

Kicking an anger emoji is another exercise to minimise anger and frustration. Tell your child to draw an anger emoji on paper, then make a ball with it and kick it. While kicking, the child should shout, 'Don't come again, just get out of my mind.' Thus, physical and mental relief can be achieved to a certain extent. This process helps children control their anger or frustration in a healthy, positive way.

- **Practise 'Deep-Breathing' exercise**

Regular practice of the 'Deep-Breathing' exercise helps control stress. So, it will be useful if a child practises the 'Deep-Breathing' exercise for one minute each day. Children should do it even when they are angry. Controlling our breathing has a significant effect on our body to reduce stress. It lowers blood pressure and heart rate. Breathing exercises are a compulsory part of stress management. The 'Deep-Breathing' exercise involves inhaling slowly through the nose and then exhaling slowly through pursed lips.

This technique is useful not only for children but also for everyone. There is no way to eliminate tantrums entirely, but there are many ways to minimise their intensity. Use these techniques to handle your little one's frustration. Some steps will work well for your child, and some may not. Always remember, parenthood is a journey of finding the correct techniques that are good for our children, and this book is an example of it.

So don't be discouraged if a technique does not work for your child; just try another one. It is simply a trial-and-error method.

Chapter 6

Motherhood Stress

Parenthood is not an easy journey. It is full of duties and responsibilities. Sometimes these burdens become so heavy that parents often suffer from stress. This parental stress has a severe effect on our children's lives. Research shows that when a pregnant mother suffers from high-stress, her fetus shows decreased functional brain activity compared to that of a mother who is less stressed. Not only the fetus but also infants through to adolescents show different symptoms when they are raised by highly stressed parents, whether it be a stressed mother or a stressed father. Children are like sponges. They absorb everything, including parental stress. So, we often see that a hyper mother has a hyper baby or a tense mother has a tense child. When stressed parents yell, either children learn to yell or they feel depressed.

Being stressed, parents often ignore their children's needs. They do not listen carefully to what their children want to say. As a result, children suffer from:

- Feelings of rejection
- Lower self-esteem
- Social withdrawal
- Disruptive and aggressive behaviour
- Sleep disturbances
- Anxiety over little things
- Depression
- Destructive behaviour towards parents or themselves
- Poor academic performance

- Poor concentration

- Irritability

But when parents show love, warmth, and care for their children, these children become more confident, happy, resilient, well-behaved, and excellent in academics and other activities, and are better able to control their emotions. They are also less likely to suffer from illness. Overall, their mental and physical growth become outstanding.

Children always want a safe and secure home where they can relax, have fun, and enjoy the warmth of togetherness. But this is not possible when there are stressed parents. Shouting, sadness, continuous worry, and anxiety cripple them. Soon, children lose the capability of thinking and the capability of speaking as well. When a child reaches adolescence, he becomes rebellious. He creates obstacles for his parents. His motto is just to disturb or annoy his parents.

A girl whose mother used to show anxiety when an exam was near tends to show anxiety about her exams too. The mother's continuous worry about exams affects her daughter badly. On the exam day, before leaving home for school, the girl would vomit; her hands would be sweaty, cold, and sometimes shaky. If her mother was somehow able to control her anxiety, then the daughter never showed such nervous behaviour. Guess who this girl is? This is me. Yes, I still suffer from such nervous behaviour. Sometimes, the effect of parental stress becomes so intense that it even continues into adulthood, as it did in my case. I am still struggling. I am very much aware that this should not happen to my little son.

So, from the beginning, I have told my son, 'An exam is nothing; it is just a process to check your brain's capability – how much your brain is able to remember. If you forget something, it is absolutely normal for the human brain. Our brain is not a computer that can store lots of information. But our brain can store information for a long time through rigorous practice, as it learns through repetition. Don't worry if you forget. We will learn it again. Just write what you can, and don't worry about what you can't.' Now my son enters the exam hall without panic.

If I show my panic about his exam, my son will definitely absorb that stress and show anxiety about the exam.

So, it is our duty to monitor our behaviour towards our children when we are under stress. If we change ourselves in response to stress, then we will be able to build a strong, positive, and happy home environment that affects not only children but also other family members. Thus, by changing ourselves, we can create a friendly environment where every family member feels safe and secure.

Remember, our harsh behaviour affects not only our children but also others around us. Harsh behaviour towards our family members due to stress does not reduce our stress level; rather, it increases it. It threatens our ability to maintain good relationships with others.

So, stress is harmful if we leave it untreated. To cope with stress, the causes of stress should be known. Until we can recognise the cause of our illness, we can't heal properly.

'Where is my toy train, Mum?' said seven-year-old Anshu. At the same time, Tina, a one-year-old girl, cried loudly. The whistling sound of the pressure cooker from the kitchen could be heard. Rabi, the father of Anshu and Tina, asked for his lunchbox as he was getting late for the office. Oh! What a horrible situation for Naina, the mother of Anshu and Tina. Yes, it is really hard work to handle all these chores. But we, the mothers, are still doing it. For a working mother, such things become more horrible to handle day by day. As a result, mothers burst into tears, frustration, and anxiety. Not only household chores create stress; there are other sources like the effects of society, social media, family members, friends, colleagues, illness, a disabled child, and so on. A new mother does not understand how to handle such stress and ends up shouting and quarrelling with her child and others.

A mother always navigates a balance between fulfilling parental duties and caring for herself. As a result, she becomes overwhelmed with stress, which impacts her physical, emotional, and mental well-being.

Here are some common triggers that create stress for mothers:

- **Feeling of not being perfect**

It is a very common and natural feeling for a mother, especially for new mothers. We often compare ourselves to other mothers and think that they are perfect. We think they raise their children flawlessly, but we can't. This unrealistic thought creates unnecessary stress on the mind. Our false belief is processed by our brain, and soon we start to act accordingly. But in reality, there is no such thing as a perfect mother. The majority of mothers face daily challenges – from chaotic moments to unexpected hurdles.

- **Social Media**

At present, teenagers and adults all spend a lot of time surfing social media like Facebook, Instagram, etc. Social media is a platform where anyone can post photos and videos, which often foster an illusion of perfection. When a mother scrolls through flawless family photos, videos, and immaculate homes, it creates unexpected demands. In reality, what we see on social media is not always true. When a mother scrolls through posts of another mother whose house is tidy, whose body shape is perfect like a model, who spends time with her child, manages her office perfectly, and even shares photos of vacations abroad, it creates huge pressure on her. We start to believe her life is smooth and struggle-free; this may be true to some extent or may not be. There may be a babysitter all the time, and she just posts photos with her child to show everything is manageable. Maybe she has a maid who does all the household chores and keeps the home clean. But we can't see such things with our bare eyes. These are the hidden truths behind the reality of social media posts. But we often ignore such things and chase for a perfect life that does not exist at all.

Mothers often follow celebrity mothers who live expensive lives. When we see Anushka Sharma at the cricket ground, we just watch her without her children. Have you ever thought about who looks after her children? If a celebrity mother is busy shooting all day long, then who takes care of her baby? Yes, they depend on maids, caregivers, or parents, which is not possible for all mothers in this world. As a result, unnecessary stress arises. Middle-class mothers don't get any free time, whether it is attending a family function or other parties. They are always busy taking care of their children.

- **Time drains and distraction created by social media**

'Oh my God, why did I surf on my mobile? I have to finish my chores,' said 28-year-old Sheela. Sheela is the mother of a one-year-old girl. When Sheela's daughter slept, she picked up her mobile, laid down, and surfed. She came to realise that she had spent a lot of time on her mobile when her daughter woke up, and she still had unfinished household chores. Soon, she was overwhelmed with stress.

This doesn't happen only to Sheela. It is a common problem for all. Mothers who suffer from a lack of time often waste time on social media. The habit of scrolling not only kills time but also impacts our minds. Today's social media content and how frequently your preferred videos or pictures appear on your mobile screen are designed in such a way that they hack our minds. Yes, social media controls us psychologically, and without realising it, we are trapped.

Many important tasks remain pending, and as a result, stress is generated. A mother has to finish work on time, so she shouts at others, complaining that no one is there to help her.

They often shout at their children for not finishing food, not wearing school uniforms, and not putting on shoes on time – tasks usually supervised by the mother. But suddenly, due to lack of time, mothers claim that these tasks can be done by their children, who are "big enough." These unexpected expectations create stress for both the children and the mothers.

- **Postpartum Depression**

Postpartum Depression is a medical condition. Many women suffer from it after giving birth. It's a strong feeling of sadness, anxiety, and tiredness. It lasts for a long period of time after having a baby. During this depression, mothers are unable to properly care for their children and themselves. Continuous mood swings, crying, anger, guilt, hopelessness, loss of interest, panic attacks, fatigue, loss of appetite, restlessness, lack of concentration, weight gain or weight loss, and insomnia are seen among mothers suffering from postpartum depression.

- **Lack of sleep**

A mother suffers from sleep deficiency with a newborn baby. Due to the feeding cycle of a newborn, a mother can't get sufficient time for rest. Due to lack of proper sleep and rest, a mother suffers from different mental health issues like frustration, depression, anxiety, worry, mood swings, and short temper. It also adversely affects health, leading to high blood pressure, stroke, obesity, diabetes, and heart disease. So, an adequate amount of sleep is needed for both physical and mental health.

Sometimes, mothers become more irritable and fatigued, lashing out at friends, co-workers, spouses, other family members, or even their children.

- **Creating Distance Between Husband and Wife**

A mother with a baby has to perform many duties. Taking care of the baby, handling office work, preparing food for the family, managing laundry, etc., are sufficient to create huge pressure on the mother, so she is unable to manage any time for her beloved husband. As a result, the distance between husband and wife increases. Yes, of course, it creates stress. Her personal life is hampered. Husbands start to see their spouses as detached, and gradually relationship problems emerge.

- **Divorce**

Divorce creates stress. Mothers who go through divorce often suffer from depression. Depression creates behavioural issues that affect children's development. Divorced mothers have to perform all the family responsibilities, and as a result, they become exhausted and frustrated, often showing their frustrations by shouting at their children. Being affected by this, children suffer from depression and lose confidence. In one word, children become mentally disabled.

- **No Self-Time**

Due to hectic schedules, mothers rarely manage 'self-time.' Most mums are unable to find any self-time. As a result, spending time with others drains energy and causes tiredness. Self-time gives energy, happiness, and peace. So, a lack of self-time means a lack of happiness, and a lack of happiness means stress. Yes, 'no self-time' creates stress.

- **Loss of loved ones**

It creates pain when someone loses loved ones. If a mother loses her parent, husband, or someone very close to her, she suffers from depression. Different physical conditions, like lack of sleep, loss of appetite, headaches, and stomachaches, are seen. Some mental issues are also observed, like lack of concentration, forgetfulness, feeling disconnected from the real world, mood swings, irritability, and so on. Naturally, when such feelings are overwhelming, mothers either burst with frustration at their children or withdraw their attention from them. Both can create a negative impact on children's minds and health.

- **Weak boundaries**

Many of us are unable to say 'No' when someone requests a favour. If this happens to a mother, then stress arises. After finishing her regular chores, a mother has to find time to fulfil others' needs. It is a very difficult task. So, mothers should practise saying 'No' when necessary. Suppose your neighbour requests you to take care of her daughter for 2 hours when your child is at school, and you are busy finishing your household work. Please say 'No'; otherwise, it will create unnecessary stress, and your neighbour's expectations will increase day by day. Don't allow your neighbour to take advantage of your inability to say 'No'. If it is urgent, then say 'Yes,' as we are social after all. Suppose you are not feeling well, but your friends insist on going shopping, and you say 'Yes' instead of 'No' because you fear isolation. This will definitely create stress, which hampers your peace of mind. Unable to handle too much stress, you end up in a mess. Your children and other family members will have to face your frustration when you outburst. So, know your limits and say 'No' without any hesitation if needed.

- **Health issues**

If health is OK, then the mind is also OK. But for a new mum, after giving birth, her health is not in proper condition as before. Besides that, sleep deprivation, not taking proper rest, not eating on time, and worrying too much can create different health issues like stomachaches, dizziness, high blood pressure, high heart rate, sweating, and hair loss. Naturally, stress is generated due to poor health conditions. Mothers lose control over their minds. I have seen many women go through gallbladder surgery a few months after having a baby. Two consecutive operations create stress. Mothers often feel guilty as they can't take proper care of their babies. They gradually sink into depression. For some women, menstruation also creates mood swings, tender breasts, food cravings, fatigue, irritability, and pain in the lower abdomen. Nowadays, it is common for mothers to suffer from low milk production during breastfeeding, which makes them feel guilty and stressed. They don't realise that it is not their fault.

- **Fear of Isolation**

Mothers often miss appointments with their friends, sometimes parties, and visits to relatives due to their babies. This creates pressure on mothers. They fear being isolated. Every relationship needs time. When you want to grow vegetables, you need time to nurture those plants. The same applies to maintaining a good relationship with others. It may be a relationship between a mother and a son, a husband and wife, a friend, or even between you and me, as you spend your valuable time reading this book. But mothers are too busy completing their daily tasks. Their hectic schedules do not allow them to find any free time for their friends and other family members, and sometimes it becomes very hard to find time to phone loved ones. As a result, the 'fear of isolation' cripples them and creates stress.

- **Finance**

Finance is a big stressor. When people go through financial problems, they suffer from depression and anxiety. Finance is a big support; it helps us to maintain a standard lifestyle. Depending on our financial condition, we decide which school we choose for our children, which health scheme we choose for our family, the 'square-foot' area of the flat we are going to buy, our vacation destination, our clothes, and so on. In one word, our lifestyle and the future of our children strongly depend on our financial condition. Nowadays, to meet the necessities of life, mums and dads are both engaged in earning money. That's why daycare centres are seen in many urban areas. The number of daycare centres increases day by day. This indicates that our financial needs are also increasing day by day.

When a mum loses her job due to pregnancy leave or during a pandemic, she faces the worst financial problems, which make her depressed. Mothers suffer from high blood pressure, high heart rate, poor sleep, headaches, stomachaches, etc., which are common physical symptoms of depression. Especially for single mothers with unsatisfying jobs or those who have lost jobs, both situations push them to the brink of depression. Yes, being unable to pay electricity bills, school fees, rent, loans, or buy food creates severe anxiety and negative thoughts that leads to the edge of stress.

- **Birth of a New Baby**

When a mum gives birth to a new baby, a sudden responsibility of a life comes upon her. If the mother gives birth to a second baby, she has to find time for both her elder child and the younger one. Sometimes, after the birth of a baby, the mother may suffer from different physical conditions, mood swings, and sleep deprivation. She has to track the proper dates of vaccinations, book appointments for regular check-ups for the newborn, and properly care for both of her children. Undoubtedly, all these responsibilities create stress for the mother.

- **Physical Illness of a Child**

If a child is physically challenged, blind, hearing-impaired, or suffers from heart problems or high diabetes, such health conditions definitely create stress for the mother.

- **No Support**

Stress arises when there is no family support. There is no one to take care of the baby when you want to go to the washroom or take a rest. I also suffer from a lack of support. I used to tie my infant's leg to the sofa with a long dupatta so that any accident could be avoided when I was in an emergency. Sometimes, I used to take my baby to the bathroom with me as well. Yes, it creates a lot of stress. When you see that your friend has great family support and you do not, it creates depression. You soon book a caregiver so that you can get some alone time. In India, the wages of caregivers are so high that some middle-class families cannot afford them. As a result, stress is generated for the mother.

- **Hectic Schedules for a Child's Activities**

We parents engage our children in multiple activities. This not only burns out our children (as I discussed earlier) but also the parents. Parents experience burnout due to the hectic schedules of their children's activities. They have to drop off and pick up their children on time. If there is traffic, commuting from home to the activity centre becomes even more time-consuming. Exhaustion and fatigue are seen in both mother and children. As a result, stress is seen among mothers. Lots of activities mean lots of time loss and exhaustion, which lead to stress.

- **Long Commute from Home to Office and Office to Home**

When the office is too far from home, you spend a lot of time commuting. It creates fatigue and exhaustion. For a woman, it is very stressful to perform her duty as a mother after a long commute. Naturally, sometimes a working mother may burst into rage.

- **Cooking**

In India, people generally cook food with vegetables combined with different spices, investing time in the process.

Preparing a sabji and rotis (handmade) requires a minimum of 30 minutes or more. If you try to cook with less oil on a chulla, it takes even more time. Indians particularly enjoy taking homemade food for lunch at the office. There are 2 reasons for this: one is that homemade food is healthy, and the other is that it saves extra money. Most Indians prefer to have roti, paratha, sabji, idli, or dosa for breakfast, and rice, dal, sabji, and fish curry for lunch. It sounds nice, but one needs a lot of time to prepare all the above-mentioned recipes. Mothers have to prepare a healthy breakfast for their children or husband, like idli, dosa, roti-sabji, or aloo-ka-paratha, and simultaneously prepare lunch, like rice, dal, fish curry, and sabji. Naturally, to complete all kitchen tasks, a mother spends 2 to 3 hours in the kitchen. It is overwhelming. To avoid cooking, some working mothers take the help of maids. Nowadays, oats, cornflakes, smoothies, etc., are preferred for breakfast, but for lunch, we still need rice, sabji, salad, and fish or egg or chicken curry instead of fast food like pizza, burgers, or Maggi, which are known to be unhealthy. Therefore, it is necessary to avoid junk food and prefer homemade food for good health, but when a mum invests her time in it, she can easily become stressed. Doctors, nutritionists, and social media constantly advocate for healthy homemade food, which pressures mothers to spend a significant amount of time to cook in kitchens where the temperature is about 40 degrees Celsius during the summer. Mothers become exhausted and irritated as they spend most of their time in a boiler-like kitchen.

Personally, I hate to cook, but I have to. When I spend 2 hours in the kitchen preparing food, and it takes hardly 15 minutes to eat it all up, I feel really exhausted and frustrated. I try new recipes from YouTube, but in the end, it only adds to my exhaustion and frustration, as I suffer from a loss of time. I know that, like me, mothers who don't prefer to cook are under stress.

- **Comparison**

We often compare ourselves to others. In the office, we compare ourselves with our colleagues. Under the influence of social media, we compare ourselves with our friends, and by doing this, we destroy our serenity. We chase things that are not suitable for us. When a child grows up being compared to others by his parents, he develops a tendency to compare himself with others in adulthood. Some adults display such behaviour, which destroys their peace of mind. Constantly chasing something that comes to mind through comparison never brings happiness. Mothers often compare themselves to other mothers, colleagues, and friends, ending up with stress, frustration, and anxiety. Mothers who compare themselves never forget to compare their children with other children, and as a result, they push their children into depression.

- **Relocation**

Because of a transferable job of the husband or herself, a mother suffers from stress. Fear of uncertainty about the workplace, home environment, and the environment of the children's school creates acute stress for mothers.

- **Domestic Violence**

Domestic violence also creates stress for mothers. This stress is so intense that it can damage the mother's or children's mental and physical health. In domestic violence, abusive behaviour is exhibited by the partner to gain or maintain power and control over another. It can include physical, sexual, emotional, economic, and psychological harassment.

Symptoms of Stress

Stress not only exhausts you but also affects your parenting. Children will grow up with an irritable, unsmiling mother.

Children will always try to keep a safe distance from the mother and learn to find comfort and emotional dependency elsewhere.

Here are some signs that indicate you are under stress. You should monitor these symptoms. When you realise you are experiencing these symptoms, you should immediately seek a solution for better parenting.

Some mental issues when you are stressed are

- Feeling of restlessness
- Lack of interest in pursuing hobbies
- Shouting at children or others without any strong reason
- Feeling irritation
- Withdrawing attention from children
- Showing lack of interest in visiting relatives' houses
- Constantly worrying about your children's future and becoming restless
- Inability to focus
- Forgetfulness or absentmindedness
- Constant bad mood or mood swings
- Frequent outbursts of rage
- Feeling of exhaustion
- Inability to enjoy yourself
- Feeling sick and dizzy
- Difficulty making decisions
- Nervousness
- Depression

Some physical symptoms of stress

- Poor sleep or even sleepless nights
- Loss of appetite or an urge to eat more
- Sudden weight gain or weight loss
- Sudden hair fall problems
- High blood pressure and high heart rate
- Frequent stomach aches, headaches, and body pain
- Sweating
- Panic attacks
- Changes to the menstrual cycle
- Trouble with sexual intimacy with a partner
- Poor digestion
- Faster breathing
- Weak immune system

Some behavioural symptoms of stress

- Regular alcohol consumption
- Starting to smoke
- Possible addiction to drugs
- Biting nails or lips
- Shopping more than usual
- Spending lots of time internet surfing

Some Strategies for Stress Relief

We cannot avoid stress, but we can handle it in a healthy way without being overwhelmed by practising some strategies:

- Practice mindfulness, which is a form of meditation that makes you aware of the present situation without judgement. It is simply a process to connect with yourself, observing one's feelings without criticism. To practise it, sit straight with closed eyes and observe what comes to mind. Don't try to control those feelings. The feelings that arise are responsible for either worry or joy. Gradually, try to focus on breathing. It is often very difficult to practise at the beginning. This technique helps to understand our present mental state and controls our minds.

- Practising exercise improves health and a sense of well-being. Physical activity promotes the production of the brain's feel-good neurotransmitters, endorphins, which naturally reduce stress. Blood flow is improved. Aerobics, swimming, jogging, and running are useful for controlling stress.

- Practising yoga is also helpful in fighting stress. Yoga binds the mind and body together. In yoga, movement, breathing, and meditation are combined. It helps to improve mood from bad to good. Practising yoga for 20 minutes each day brings the blessing of good health and peace of mind.

- Sometimes, it is necessary to say 'no' to extra responsibilities. It provides a feeling of self-control and helps you to manage time for yourself.

- Spending quality time with your partner gives a sense of relaxation. It not only improves bonding between you and your partner but also helps to reduce stress.

- Try to manage time to go to a spa or salon. Give yourself a special treatment to feel that you are also special. Treat yourself with affection. If necessary, request your partner to take care of your child so that you can enjoy your spa time.

- You have to feel that you are special. Your self-approval matters a lot to reduce stress. So, please don't hesitate to ask your husband or other family members to take care of your baby so that you can get 'me-time'. You deserve 'me-time'. During 'me-time', you can sleep, listen to music, read books, dance, walk, swim and do anything that you truly want to do. Just do the activity that gives you fresh oxygen to breathe well in a suffocating world.

- A hobby is always close to the heart. It gives happiness. Pursuing a hobby is always helpful for a mother to reduce stress hormones and increase the happy hormone, dopamine, in the body.

- Always remember, you don't get any help until you ask for it. So, don't hesitate—if you're tired, just ask other family members to help you finish household chores more quickly. Remember, it is not only your duty to keep the home clean and tidy. Other members of the home have the same responsibilities.

- Stop trying to be perfect. Yes, your expectation of becoming 'perfect' creates unnecessary stress. Always remember, no one is perfect. If someone can be a good cook, then she may not be a perfect singer. If someone is talented in painting, she may not be a good swimmer. In Japan, people believe in 'wabi-sabi,' which means finding beauty in imperfection.

- One of the best ways to kick stress out of our lives is to stay away from social media and focus on what we have and what we want. Yes, I felt a lot of stress when I engaged with social media. I became depressed when I saw a woman who efficiently managed her entrepreneurship journey and motherhood. I thought, 'How is it possible?' I mentioned before, what we see is what others show us. So, I soon completely cut myself off from social media; it has been at least 2 years now, and as a result, I published my first competitive exam book and am now busy finishing this book. Now, I am a proud mother of a little eight-year-old son and am very happy thinking that this book may help many parents in their bleak situations.

- To manage stress, you should read a positive book that can change your life. Don't worry; it's not a bad idea. Some books have completely changed my life. I started to read life-changing books when my son was just one and a half years old. At that time, I was very depressed because I had already left my job, had no money in hand, no help at home to raise my son, and no financial freedom. I was preparing for government jobs but was unable to find free time. My husband helped me a lot in that situation, but I still wanted to be self-dependent. There seemed to be no way, no light. One day, my husband bought a book, *The Monk Who Sold His Ferrari* by Robin Sharma, and my life changed. It is also true that a book alone cannot completely change your life unless you want it desperately. Changing your life requires courage.

  I have read many life-changing books and finally found my purpose: to help people who are depressed and to raise my son through positive parenting.

- Prioritising sleep is necessary if you want to be stress-free. Yes, a minimum of 8 hours of sleep is needed to maintain a healthy body and mind.

- Physical irritation creates stress. You cannot be happy if your health does not allow it. So, if you feel any physical irritation, consult a doctor. Just fix the problem. If your physical condition can be improved naturally, then follow that path instead of taking unnecessary medicines, as medicines have some side effects too. For instance, to reduce migraine, you should avoid foods that trigger it, get adequate sleep and rest, and avoid harsh situations that may worsen your migraine. You can take medication as per your doctor's advice, but first try to heal naturally.

- You will get free time depending on your time management skills. For example, just cook one sabji and rotis instead of 2 vegetable curries (sabji). The time saved by not cooking the second dish becomes your free time. During this time, you could dance, for instance.

- Plan for a vacation in a quiet place, preferably in the lap of nature. Nature heals us.

- When stressed, mothers shout at their children, then swear not to shout again, but the next morning, they break their promise. To avoid this, write down "Be Calm and Talk Politely" and stick it on the wall of the room where you spend the most time. This reminder helps you to keep your promise. It influences your brain to act according to the instructions on the wall. I tried this, and soon I noticed a subtle change in myself.

- When relatives or friends visit your house and offer help, accept it if you feel exhausted. There is nothing wrong with accepting their help.

- Lastly, engage yourself in a small mum group in your community (if possible). It gives you strength and shows that you are not the only one struggling. Some advice from other mothers may help you nurture your child in a better way. Accept advice with maturity; take on board what you think suits you and disregard what doesn't.

- At last, if you think expertise is required to help you mentally, physically, and financially, then go ahead without hesitation. It's your life, and you have the freedom to be happy and to enjoy a good, healthy life.

Motherhood is an excellent experience for a woman. It has lots of ups and downs, but still, it is joyful. When a fat woman starts exercising and follows a strict diet to shape her body, and at last, when she gets the result, she is in ecstasy. Now she is not fat anymore; she is slim. Like this fat woman, mothers have to suffer a lot of pain, but at last, they feel the same ecstasy as the fat woman did.

Suppose you plant a sapling. Regularly, you take care of it by giving it water, manure, or fertiliser, and protect it from cattle. You also ensure that your sapling gets proper sunlight for photosynthesis. After 3 to 4 years, you will see your little sapling has transformed into a big tree which does not need any more care from you and gives you mangoes to eat. Now, this is the result of your proper nourishment. Your little sapling is now self-sufficient. The same happens to a mother when she finds her little one has transformed into a confident, self-sufficient person who is capable of handling the harsh world with ease. At that time, she gets the sweetest fruit of motherhood.

Motherhood is not a destination; it is a life-changing journey. Enjoy every moment of it.

Chapter 7

Fatherhood Troubles

Fatherhood is an incredible journey of life, like motherhood. When a father holds his baby for the first time, he is overwhelmed with emotion. Such a feeling is indescribable. But fatherhood also brings some stress, as we can see in a mother's life. We often overlook the stress and pain of a father. Our society views a father as strong, stoic, and emotionless. Society teaches us to ignore a father's pain and assumes that a father can handle such stress efficiently without showing it to others. Yes, this is true to some extent. I have seen my father wake up early in the morning. Next, he dropped me at school, bought vegetables, ate breakfast, and went out for his office. I saw his tired face after 7 p.m. After returning home, he used to play with me and my brother or help us to complete our homework and then took dinner and slept. It was his daily routine. In this busy schedule, he had no 'me-time' or 'fun-time.'

Fathers perform their duties without complaining. They are expected to provide financial and emotional support to their families. This high expectation can be overwhelming, particularly if a father's own upbringing did not prepare him for this role. As a result, stress is generated.

Here are some causes responsible for a father's stress:

- **Work-life Balance**

Maintaining a balanced work-life can be difficult for fathers, as most fathers think that providing strong financial support to their family is the primary goal in life. So, they ignore family and suffer from guilt and anxiety. They make themselves too busy focusing on finance, so they rarely manage good quality time to spend with their families.

- ### Shrinking Finance

Finance is sufficient to create stress in anyone's life, and fathers are no exception. All responsibilities of a family are on a father's shoulders. They always look out for better opportunities to enhance their financial stability. When a father joins a new venture, pressure arises automatically, and stress hormones start to circulate in his body. So, worry about finance often creates stress, and sometimes fathers suffer from high blood pressure and diabetes.

- ### Long Commuting

Long commuting from home to office and office to home creates exhaustion, which leads to frustration and, ultimately, stress. Due to long commuting time, a father cannot manage any free time, and stress appears in his life.

- ### Social Expectations

As I have mentioned, our society tells us that fathers are strong both mentally and physically. So, the pressure to suppress emotion can have the worst effect on mental health, leading to anxiety, depression, and burnout.

- ### Health Issues

If we are sick, then we fail to connect with our tasks, and we feel stress. The same happens to fathers. Sickness takes away happiness from our lives and leaves us with worry and depression.

- ### Worry about Family

In some families, the father is the only breadwinner. A father carries all the responsibility for his family. He works hard just to provide a good, comfortable life to all family members. So, naturally, stress is generated. When there is a disabled member in the family, the stress level triples.

- **Worry about the Future of the Child**

We see fathers as strong, robust, and worriless. But, in reality, concern about a child's future creates stress. High population and unemployment among the younger generation often create a high level of stress. Worry about securing a child's future often causes fathers to have sleepless nights.

- **No Family Support**

Having no support from family also creates stress. When a father finds himself helpless and unsupported both financially and emotionally by his family, stress hormones start to release. Some fathers who cook after completing their office work and help their children with studies are not able to find any 'me-time.' As a result, they suffer from depression and short temper.

Yes, like mothers, fathers also need 'me-time' for self-recharging. When a father is criticised by other family members, unnecessary toxic stress is generated.

- **Extra Responsibilities in a Nuclear Family**

Helping a spouse to finish household chores is a common task for a man after his office hours. Taking care of a child is another hectic job, which a man does efficiently with a smiling face. There is no one to whom he can complain or request relief for relaxation. In India, these are very common problems for men who live in another city for work. Extra responsibilities cripple them mentally and physically, leaving them exhausted and stressed.

- **Trouble Maintaining Good Relationships with Others**

Maintaining a good relationship with others requires time. Time is the only key to maintaining a strong bond. But a breadwinner father is hardly able to manage time to spend with his family. So, it weakens the bonding between him and his spouse, children, and other family members. To establish a strong relationship with children, it is necessary to play with them, talk to them, and plan small trips. But a busy father often forgets or sometimes intentionally ignores this, and later fears about not having a good relationship with his child. This creates stress for fathers in later life.

A positive relationship with a spouse is also necessary to raise a positive child. A toxic relationship destroys a child's mental development. Besides that, fathers who suffer from relationship problems with their spouse often experience anxiety and depression.

- **Lack of Sleep**

Sleep is necessary to maintain good health and mental stability. If sleep is hampered, stress is generated in the human body. Especially when you have a newborn baby, it is often difficult to have sound sleep at night. Besides that, after returning home, a man helps his spouse complete household chores and spends time with the children. These activities reduce sleep time. As a result, stress hormones are secreted.

- **Losing Friends**

As I already mentioned, every relationship needs time. After becoming a father or husband, a man often becomes confined to family life and hardly manages time to hang out with friends. Men often decline friends' invitations due to tiredness, family obligations, or simply a lack of time. Naturally, their circle of friends shrinks. They begin to lose friends one by one and suffer from anxiety and depression. Sometimes, they isolate themselves entirely from their friends, creating additional pressure.

- **Social Media**

Social media is powerful enough to create stress in people's lives. Yes, with the advent of social media, men, like women, are also suffering from stress, anxiety, and depression.

The 'image of being perfect' affects men too. Some men believe what they see on social media is true. But, in reality, most videos and pictures are edited and dramatised. Men may be surprised by what they see on social media—how a man can handle family life, professional life, and his friends effortlessly. Like women, men are also equally involved in social media to display their lifestyle. Sometimes it is seen that a man enjoys multiple professions simultaneously and lives a lavish life. There is no doubt that when a man observes such things on social media, he may sink into depression.

Always remember, what we see is not necessarily true. On social media, a person who inspires jealousy may be living with difficulties that are not shown. So, before harming health and mental stability, one should inspect the truth behind situations that create a negative impact.

- **Relocation**

Shifting from one place to another often creates stress for a father. A father worries about the new environment in his children's school, the neighbours around him, the conditions in the locality surrounding his house, and adjusting to a new office.

Symptoms of a Father's Stress

Like mothers, fathers also experience stress. It is observed that 1 out of 10 new dads can experience depression during their spouse's pregnancy or after having a baby. Fathers often ignore their depression as they are not always open about it. If a father's depression is left untreated, it can adversely affect his health and mind. A father's mental health has a significant impact on his child's development and well-being.

Here are some symptoms of depression in men:

- Tiredness, feeling exhausted

- Yelling at children and sometimes at spouse as well

- Irritability, anxiety, and anger

- Sudden outbursts of rage

- Changes in appetite

- Feeling overwhelmed and unable to cope

- Loss of libido

- Suffering from sleep deprivation

- Feeling isolated from family, child, and friends

- Feeling disconnected from partner and children

- Withdrawing attention from family

- Addiction to alcohol and cigarettes

- Absent-mindedness

- Forgetfulness

- Gaining weight and showing less interest in self-care

- Addiction to gambling

- Experiencing muscle jerks

- Increasing blood pressure and developing diabetes

- Frequent headaches

- Developing itchy skin and sweating problems

Stress Management for Dads

As I mentioned earlier, children are like sponges and are ready to absorb everything happening around them. They keenly observe how their parents talk to each other, how they interact with friends or others, how they shout at them when stressed, and so on. So, it is necessary to raise a child in a positive and stress-free environment. When a child is raised in a stressful environment, he easily learns how to become stressed. The child sees only the negative side of every situation. The same happened to me—not because of my dad, but because of my mother. My mum worried about my future, and as a result, I picked up the habit of stress and forgot to enjoy my life. I spent most of my time thinking about my future. It's really suffocating. So, like mothers, fathers need special care. There is no shame if a father admits he is stressed. He is not God; he is a human being, and stress can appear in anyone's life regardless of gender. To establish a strong bond with the child and to improve the child's cognitive development, a father should take care of himself. If he feels he needs help, he should seek it. Establishing good mental health is necessary for both a father and a child. Remember, mental stability also helps to bring happiness to life.

Here Are Some Tips to Control Fatherhood Stress:

- **Try to Build Healthy Habits**

First, promise yourself not to yell at others. Get enough sleep. Don't drink too much alcohol, and try not to smoke. Finally, make time for physical activity (exercise). Initially, these tasks may seem difficult to carry out, but with willpower, you can convert them into new habits and see the benefits. These healthy habits will definitely bring happiness, confidence, and calmness to your life.

- **Schedule Fun**

To keep stress away, it is necessary to schedule regular time to do things that you truly enjoy. It could be swimming, going out with friends, having a date with your spouse or enjoying a head massage.

- **Follow a Hobby**

Manage a little time to follow your hobby. If playing guitar is your hobby, then just play guitar on the weekend. Hobbies help to provide happiness and keep stress out of our lives.

- **Stop Comparing**

Subconsciously, we often compare ourselves with others, and fathers are no exception. So, consciously pay attention to this habit. The more you compare yourself to others, the more stress will be generated. It will definitely hamper mental stability. Always believe that you are unique. Your journey is not the same as those you may feel envious of.

- **Stop Surfing Social Media Unnecessarily**

Social media takes over valuable time, and after spending one to 2 hours on it, you may feel worthless for wasting that time. Unnecessary social media browsing creates stress. On social media, seeing something or someone and constantly thinking about it only pushes you into a dark, distressing space. So, it is good for you and your family to stay away from social media. It also causes distraction and poor concentration. If a father is addicted to social media, there is a probability that his child will become addicted to it during a crucial time in life.

- **Eat Healthy**

Healthy eating habits enhance our mood and health. So, to reduce stress, it is necessary to avoid junk food and develop good, healthy eating habits. You can eat oats, fruits, veggies, rice, daal, roti, fish curry, and so on. Try to avoid too much coffee as it increases blood pressure and affects sleep.

- **Practice Mindfulness and Breathing Yoga**

Mindfulness is the practice of gently focusing on the present moment, creating a feeling of calmness. Initially, it may be difficult, but with continuous practice, it becomes easier and helps control stress.

Some breathing yoga exercises, like Anulom-Vilom, Bhramari, Balasana, and Savasana, help reduce stress. Try to practise yoga for at least 20 minutes daily.

- **Ask for Help**

Say goodbye to gender roles when it comes to asking for help. Men are taught not to ask for help, thinking they can manage on their own. But, in reality, everyone, including men, needs help to cope with stress. If men don't ask for help from their spouse or parents, they invite unnecessary stress into their lives. So, don't hesitate, dads. Just ask for help if needed. It is not a sign of weakness. It will help you to be a great dad.

- **Talk to Your Partner**

Talk with your partner about your stress at work and your happiness. This method reduces stress caused by domestic quarrelling, and undoubtedly, it improves bonding between you and your partner. Your wife will feel special when you open up to her, and she will be more affectionate towards you.

- **Attend Parental Classes**

Parental classes can help a father learn about the delivery process, a mother's mood swings, postpartum issues, the challenges of being a new father, how to care for a newborn baby, and more. Consult a professional who can help to clarify any doubts about your fatherhood journey, which may help reduce stress.

- **Maintain a routine**

Try to maintain a routine. It helps ensure that you are setting aside 'me-time' for self-care.

- **Join a father group**

When a father joins a father group, he understands that not only he, but other fathers are also suffering from the same problems. All fathers face the same challenges as a new father does. From this group, a father can pick up good advice to maintain a healthy, balanced life.

- **Make a Financial Plan**

If you find it difficult to manage your money when a new responsibility is on your shoulders, try consulting a financial consultant. You can also handle your finances or, better to say, make a good financial plan for your future to support your family by researching on the internet, in books, newspapers, etc. This gives you a feeling of a secure future and helps to reduce stress.

It is necessary to take your wife on the same financial path because balance is needed from both sides. When your wife understands the struggle, she will definitely help you save extra money.

- **Say 'No' if necessary**

Sometimes it is necessary to say 'No', especially when you are overwhelmed by your new responsibilities. Building healthy boundaries helps reduce stress. For instance, after returning home from the office, if you are exhausted and your spouse requests you to go to the market, just say 'No'.

Rest is required for both your body and mind. Instead of going to the market, tell your wife that you are physically exhausted, need some rest, and suggest planning to go on the next holiday to spend the whole time together. Quality time is also needed to reduce stress, after all.

- **Keep in touch with a doctor**

If there is a physically challenged child in the family, then a father should maintain good communication with the doctor and follow his advice. This provides a sense of secure parental care. Try to join a group of fathers who are also dealing with similar challenges. This will provide mental stability and help you realise you are not the only one facing these issues.

- **Listen to music**

Music has a soothing power to relieve stress. So, listening to music to reduce stress is necessary.

Fatherhood is a rewarding journey, but it is also full of stress, frustrations, and challenges. There are many obstacles that a father has to face and manage. There is no definition of a 'perfect father'. Through facing unique challenges, one gradually develops the skills needed for fatherhood. Always remember, fathers are the umbrella for children. They protect them from dangers and make them resilient enough to face the world awaiting them.

Chapter 8

Some Practical Problems With Solutions

How to cope with a stubborn child

A child goes through different physical and mental transformations each year, and these changes make him somewhat stubborn. Instead of fighting with the child, parents can handle this situation by following these steps:

- Try to understand what triggers your child and work to avoid those situations.

- Parents often say 'NO' to their child parents often show their power over child. These things make child mad. The child suffers from depression and anxiety, and sometimes, he becomes rigid in his decisions just to show his existence and importance. So, try not to say 'NO' to everything with your child and treat him as if they have value in the family. Give importance to child's opinions.

- Listen to your child carefully; otherwise, your child will think that you ignore him, and soon he will start to show his rigidity.

- If your child tries to defy you in trivial things, like wanting to wear a pink dress but you insist on a green one, just let her choose as she wants. It provides a sense of self-control and independence. It helps to make her happy. Don't give too many options to choose from, as it may overwhelm her.

- Don't engage the child in more than one activity. A child becomes exhausted due to too many activities and may have emotional outbursts.

- Don't compare your child with other children. It creates feelings of being ignored, unwanted, and unloved. So, the child becomes rebellious.

- Always talk with affection.

- When a child screams to get a desired thing, and you buy it for him, he learns that screaming is necessary to get what he wants. As a result, he starts to show more stubbornness. When you are in public, wait until your child calms down.

How to deal with a lying child

Basically, one starts to tell lies when one feels that if he speaks the truth, he will be scolded, insulted, or punished. Fear of insult and punishment compels one to lie. We can see this frequently between husband and wife, just to avoid conflict. So, our little one is not the exception.

Here are some steps to help you handle your little one controlling his habit of lying:

- When your child acknowledges his fault, then please, please, don't scold him. Rather, praise him for speaking the truth. Later, gently teach him that what he has done is wrong and that you never expect it to happen again. Everyone wants to take shelter in a safe place when they have done wrong. The same happens to our children, and parents are the best shelter for any child. This method helps your child to feel secure and learn the difference between right and wrong.

- A child can adopt the habit of lying from school friends or playmates. Handle this situation delicately. It is better to tell your child that lying is a bad habit and that no one will trust them in the future, or perhaps tell the childhood story 'The Shepherd and the Wolf'.

- Parents also should stop lying to each other in front of their child.

- Build a strong mental bond with your child so that both of you can trust each other.

How to deal with an electronically addicted child

To afford home rent, school fees, electricity bills, car EMI, etc., it is necessary to earn enough money. So, nowadays, both mum and dad earn money. When they return home exhausted, they have no interest in playing with their children, and to get some relaxed 'me-time', parents engage children with digital screens like television, mobile phones, and computers. Not only for working mothers; this is also applicable to non-working mothers. It is often seen that mothers engage themselves too much in surfing the internet. So, they often ignore or deny spending quality time with their children. As a result, mothers engage their children with television and mobile devices so they can surf the internet with ease.

A child cannot handle any electronic gadget until he knows how to handle it. There is no need to say that parents hand over gadgets to their children. Here are some steps to cut down screen time.

- It is necessary for parents to set a boundary on screen time for children.

- Parents are also encouraged to cut down their own mobile surfing time.

- Engage your child in physical activity.

- Engage yourself in play with your child.

- Don't allow screens while eating.

- Switch off all electronic gadgets 3 hours before bedtime, as it disrupts the sleep cycle.

- When visiting relatives, encourage your child to play with others instead of watching a mobile screen. This helps to socialise children.

How to handle fighting between siblings

Parents often feel tension when 2 siblings fight each other. To avoid or control sibling fights, here are some steps to follow:

- Parents should intervene as soon as siblings start arguing. This can prevent escalation.

- Before giving your opinion, parents should scrutinise the matter thoroughly; otherwise, there may be a risk of bias.

- Evaluate every situation impartially. Otherwise, your younger child might feel you prioritise the elder one, or vice versa.

- Teach your younger child to speak politely to his elder brother (or sister).

- Teach your elder child to forgive his little brother (or sister) for mistakes, as the younger child may be unable to think as clearly.

- Teach your children to share. This can help avoid conflicts between them. Don't take one side in every situation. For example, if you scold your elder son instead of the younger son each time, he may feel blamed, causing resentment towards both you and his sibling. Later in life, you may face sibling rivalry that you cannot manage with your rebellious elder son.

- Give your elder child the responsibility of looking after his younger sibling when you are busy in the kitchen. This helps develop a sense of responsibility in your elder child, reduces fighting, and strengthens their bond.

How to handle a fighting child

Complaints are continuously coming from school that your son hit his friend. You are frustrated and scold him. You repeatedly request him to behave properly but see no improvement. In this situation, you need to consider the psychology behind his behaviour.

Main causes behind it are:

- First is that you beat your son too often. Whatever mistake he has done, you beat him. I know you don't do it intentionally. There are lots of family and office pressure on your head, and you become impatient and beat him for his mistake. Your child learns it from you and applies it to school friends and other playmates. When my son was in pre-school, there was a boy named Tojo, who used to beat every child, and all parents complained about it to teachers. Lastly, I came to know from his mother that she beat him for every mistake he had done. She thought those mistakes were intolerable. She also acknowledged that she had to do all the household chores, which were very frustrating to her. She had to cook different items according to the demands of each family member. So, this is a simple sign of motherhood stress. Instead of beating, let your child explore everything himself, and if there is something wrong, just speak with him and discuss it with him.

- When a father beats a mother, it has an adverse effect on the child's mental growth. The child thinks he can do it with others and that there is nothing wrong. So, you silently send a wrong message to your child.

- Parents should stop domestic violence, stop quarrelling with each other, and stop beating children. In some countries, beating children is a crime, and there is punishment for this offence.

- When your child witnesses any fighting among children in the school car, school classroom, or playground. Being like a sponge, your child absorbs it and applies it at school or another place.

- If your son is bullied, then talk with teachers immediately. When a child is bullied in school, he becomes either ferocious or depressed.

- Sometimes children act according to their favourite cartoon heroes like Chhota Bheem, Superman, Spiderman, and so on. Keep a watch on the programmes they prefer to watch. It's better to sit with your child and watch the programme together. In this way, you can be sure whether the cartoon affects his behaviour or not. If it does, then stop him from watching it further.

So, to control the rage of your child, you should address the cause behind it.

How to handle bad habits of a child

Nail-biting, lip-biting, sucking a finger, pulling hair, chewing objects like pencils, pens, erasers, making faces, blinking eyes abnormally, etc., are common bad habits seen among children.

There are mainly 3 causes behind it, and they are:

First, when children are in stress, they develop different bad habits. They often pick up bad habits like nail-biting, finger-biting, and sucking a finger. They do this as such things soothe them. The second cause is boredom. Some children are seen biting their nails while they are watching television. It is not a state of anxiety. The third cause is when children mimic someone who has some bad habits. Suppose a child spends a lot of time with his caregiver, and the caregiver has a habit of picking the inside of cheeks (cheek-biting), and soon you observe that child mimics that habit.

You are a role model for your child. Before searching for the true cause of your child's bad habits, ask yourself whether it is one of your bad habits or not.

So, to control it, you may follow the steps:

- Gently remind your child that what he is doing is a bad habit, and he should not do it.

- Some habits automatically disappear with time. If it is not, then tell him politely that no one likes bad habits, and he should not do it. Explain also the bad effects of those bad habits.

- When children are bored and develop bad habits, encourage them to do something like painting, crafting, playing with Legos, etc. It helps to divert their minds from developing bad habits.

- If there is anxiety or stress behind any bad habits, then you have to deal with the stress. Find the cause of stress and assure children that they can solve problems with ease. Tell them there is nothing to worry too much about; every problem has a solution.

How to deal with a rudely spoken child

When you see your child talks rudely to you and others, you should take the matter more seriously. A child learns everything from the world. He does not come to the earth with such knowledge. So, how to talk with others is a skill that is developed in early childhood. If children see parents talk to each other rudely, or mum talks rudely to others, then they learn this way of talking. It may not be you; it may be others who influence the way your child talks. Basically, a child picks up the habits of those with whom he spends the most time. Parents, teachers, caregivers, and grandparents are those who spend the most time with children.

My son once developed this habit. His class teacher was too noisy and scolded and shouted at every child. I saw that when he returned home, he used to shout at me and talked rudely. But, on Saturday and Sunday, he talked normally as those 2 days were holidays. It was also seen that when I was disturbed, I also talked rudely, and soon my son picked up that habit. To reduce it, I started to talk politely, and as a result, my son soon picked up this habit. Besides that, when my son was promoted to the next class, he started to speak politely after returning home from school. So, when you deal with your child, it is necessary to keep your voice low and polite and remind him that he is talking rudely and you never expect it from him. A good boy always talks to everyone politely. With your true patience, soon your child recovers from the bad habit of talking rudely.

Resources

"What Are 4 types of Child Personalities?" by Karthik Kumar, MBBS; medicinenet.com

"Parenting: Understanding Your Child's Nature" by Mike Jackson, (May28,2014); goodtherapy.org.

"How to Deal With Indecision When You're an Introvert who overthinks", by Marissa Dike, (March 10, 2021); introvertdear.com.

"A neuroscientist shares the 4'highly coveted' skills that set introverts apart: 'Their brains work differently'", by Friederike Fabritius, (February 7, 2023); cnbc.com.

"What Are Introverts Like as Children? Here Are 7 Common Characteristics", by Jenn Granneman, (January 26,2024); introvertdear.com

"Signs You Might Be an Extrovert", by Kendra Cherry, (June 27, 2024); verywellmind.com

"How to Nurture Your Child As An Introvert or Extrovert." by Koni Garofalo and Michelle Schmidt (January 14, 2021); childsavers.org.

"Tips for Managing Your Extroverted Child", by Ruby Oliver, (July 152023); wehavekids.com.

"The Brain, Emotions and Behaviours", (14/07/2017); changepsychology.com.

"The Psychological Comforts of Storytelling For Kids", by Matan Guttman, (April 25, 2022); getzoo.com.

"Why storytelling may be the secret to success at work", by Harvey Deutschendorf, (10-17-2023); fastcompany.com.

"THE PERFECT STORY" by Kare Eber; Publisher: Harper Horizon.

"Emotion in stories gets our attention- and attention affects our memories", by Max Witynski, (Aug 16, 2021); uchicago.edu.

"THE COURAGRE TO BE DISLIKED", 'THE THIRD NIGHT, Discard other people's tasks' by ICHIRO KISHIMI and FUMITAKE KOGA; Publisher: Allen & Unwin.

"What is Self- Reliance and How to Develop It?", by Catherine Moore, (15 Apr, 2019); positivepsychology.com.

"The Important of teaching Kids to Be Self-Reliant" by kjohnson@haymarketca.com, (May 21, 2021); haymarketca.com.

"Free to LEARN" by Peter Gray. Publisher: Basic Books, 1st edition (1 January, 2015).

"Stress in childhood: MedlinePlus Medical Encyclopedia"; medlineplus.gov.

"What to know about stress in children" by Beth Sissons (December 20, 2023) and reviewed by Akilah Reynolds; medicalnewstoday.com.

"What Are The Different Types Of Stress?" (Jun 21, 2022); selectpsychology.co.uk.

"THE HAPPY KID HANDBOOK" by KATIE HURLEY; Publisher: TARCHER PENGUIN.

"THE WHOLE-BRAIN CHILD" BY DANIEL J. SIEGEL, M.D. and TINA PAYNE BRYSON, PhD.; Publisher: BANTAM BOOKS.

"brain rules" by JOHN MEDINA; Publisher: Pear press.

"Stress and your health"; medlineplus.gov.

"3 Types of Stress: Causes, Effects, & How to Cope" by Davina Tiwari, MSW, RSW, CSFT and Medical Reviewer: Kristen Fuller, MD; (November 6, 2023); choosingtherapy.com.

"What is chronic stress and what are its common health impacts?" by Aaron Kandola and Alina Sharon, reviewed by Nicole Washington, (September 3, 2024); medicalnewstoday.com.

"Noise and stress: a comprehensive approach" by J C Westman, J R Walters, Environmental Health Perspective, Vol. 41, pp. 291-309, 1981; pmc.ncbi.nlm.nih.gov.

"Childhood Stress: How Parents Can Help" Medically reviewed by: Zachary Radcliff, PhD Psychology (September 2023); kidshealth.com.

"Childhood Stress and Development"; lumenlearning.com.

"Effect of Bullying" by stopbullying.gov.

"The Mental Health Impact of Bullying on Kids and Teens" by mcleanhospital.org.

"Fear of rejection: What it is and how to overcome it", Written by Mandy French and reviewed by Kendra Kubala, PsyD, Psychology, (February 16, 2024); medicalnewstoday.com.

"How to Help Kids Deal With Rejection" by Katherine Prudente; childmind.org.

"Economic Stress in the Family and Children's Emotional and Behavioural Problems" by DAVID T. TAKEUCHI, University of California; DAVID R. WILLIAMS, Yale University; RUSSEL K. ADAIR, Yale University; Journal of Marriage and Family 53 (November 1991): 1031-1041; https://www.jstor.org/stable/3530

"Is melatonin a helpful sleep aid — and what should I know about melatonin side effects?" by Brent Bauer; mayoclinic.org.

"Brain derived neurotrophic factor and its clinical implications", by Siresha Bathina and Undurti N Das; pmc.ncbi.nlm.nih.gov.

"Sibling Rivalry", Reviewed by Sara Marie Laule; mottchildren.org.

"Recognizing Anxiety Symptoms in Children" by Sara Lindberg (June 9, 20210) and reviewed by Akilah Reynolds; healthline.com.

"All About Family Stress" by Karen Lamoreux, reviewed by Jennifer Litner, (April 7, 2022); psychcentral.com.

"Family stress: An evidence based guide" by Gwen Dewar; parentingscience.com.

"Understanding and Managing Mom Stress", Jan 2024; susanlandersmd.com.

"Father's Day Special: Silent struggles of working dads" by Carina Kohli, (Jun 15, 2023); wionews.com.

"The Invisible Burden: Understanding the Stress of Fathers", (Mar 29, 2023); medium.com.

"What causes parental anxiety and what effects does it have?" by Adam Rowden (April 27, 2022), reviewed by Akilah Reynolds; medicalnewstoday.com.

"Parental stress", Reviewed by Cari Michaels, 2023; extension.umn.edu.

"How Parental Stress Can Affect a Child's Health", by Vanessa LoBue, Ph.D., The baby Scientist, (March 7, 2022); psychologytoday.com.

"Parenting Stress and its Impacts", (June 6, 2023); thrive.psu.edu.

"Postpartum depression", (March,2019); marchofdimes.org.

"Managing fatherhood stress"; cope.org.

"Stress Management Techniques & Strategies to Deal with Stress", Lawrence Robinson and Melinda Smith, M.A; helpguide.org.

"Understanding Sleep Deprivation and New Parenthood", by Dr. Carly Snyder and Danielle Pacheco, (August 10, 2023); sleepfoundation.org.

www.ingramcontent.com/pod-product-compliance
Lightning Source LLC
Chambersburg PA
CBHW022020150726
47990CB00002B/734